Eternal Springs

Joy Found in the Book of John

Bruce Floren

For information, contact

MSI Press, LLC
1760-F Airline Hwy #203
Hollister, CA 95023

Copyeditor: Betty Lou Leaver
Cover design & layout: Opeyemi Ikuborije

ISBN: 978-1-957354-90-3
LCCN: 2026906862

CONTENTS

To Mason and Mila, and any other
Grandchildren who follow

Introduction

Considering the times and the emotional climate of our country, a book about personal joy might seem out of place, even trivial, unless it were to give context in relation to the whole. This book, then, should not only be personally instructive concerning one's inner life but should also be relevant to everyone's communal experience, given this current time of division and deep conviction when everyone is claiming God to be on their side. We all have a circle of influence and a responsibility to witness. The thrust of my perspective is that personal peace, assurance, vitality, and joy are gifts from God. They are not ends in themselves but are given so that we may have strength to love all people. The Hebrew concept of Shalom is the heart of the matter—inner peace in a communal environment of justice and harmony. People should not look at us and surmise that we are good. Rather, our story should be an ongoing testimony about God's goodness. This book is a call to self-examination, whichever your side might be. Exhibiting God's love is the goal, and peacemaking is my ambition. Loving people can be hard, especially when they represent opposition. Operating out of a deep-seated place of peace, love, vitality, and joy without being reactionary presents a challenge. Love should not be a legalistic experience of duty. Rather, God wants to instill in us deep heartfelt compassion. Genuine love emanates from the joy that God gives. It reflects God's power to work miracles in a fallen world.

Love through joy expresses the spirit of God's law: "to act justly and to love mercy and to walk humbly with your God" (Micah 6:8). Walking humbly acknowledges that God knows all and that "I" in my finite and sometimes flawed perspective can be wrong. As compassionate human beings, we need to at least start with the fair assessment that others are equally competent in making meaning of their own lives and drawing adequate conclusions. Understandably, we sometimes see things differently; there are some seven billion different sets of experience across the world. So, in choosing between perspectives, we need to be circumspect. The human tendency is to think that somehow, *we* are more just, more capable of seeing truth, or better equipped at getting it right. Instead of looking to God, *we* want to be gods onto ourselves. In arrogance, we force our own sense of reality on others creating a rift, divisions, and strife. God did not intend it to be so. He knows that the burden of judgement is too heavy for individuals. It twists and contorts and disfigures individual souls. That is why Christ came! He relieves us of harsh emotions and burdensome judgements and invites us to just come and follow. He taught, and he led by example. Joy is for those who faithfully submit to him.

With that said, I freely admit that this book is not an interpretation of the Gospel of John. One class of Greek in seminary by no means made me fluent in its nuances nor skilled at translation. Like most, I depend on the acumen of the experts. In my studies, I have come to depend on their serious labor. I trust that the original message has been well handled and that what is generally accepted as Scripture aligns well with the intended meaning of its authors. In this, Scripture is miraculously consistent, resulting in God's Word that is

> alive and active. Sharper than any double-edged sword, it penetrates even to dividing soul and spirit, joints and marrow; it judges the thoughts and attitudes of the heart (Hebrews 4:12).[1]

Isaiah writes,

> As the rain and the snow come down from heaven, and do not return to it without watering the earth and making it bud and flourish, so that it yields seed for the Sower and bread for the eater, so is

---

1. All Bible references use the *New International Version, Zondervan NIV Study Bible* (K. L. Barker, Ed.; Full rev. ed.). (2002). Zondervan.

> my word that goes out from my mouth: It will not return to me empty, but will accomplish what I desire and achieve the purpose for which I sent it (55:10-11).

Like no other book, the Bible was remarkably conceived, living up to its reputation as the inspired word of God. The Bible inspires awe and reverence in me and has become my backbone and strength, consolation, and joy in matters of life and living. I hope it will become the same for you.

This book is not intended as a commentary; you will find no references or formalities. I prefer a free flow of thought, not aspiring to high levels of dry and tiresome academics. In speaking to those whom I love, I prefer plain language. I care about your success. I care about you. I aim to share my learned experience merely as a sort of practical application to my life from the book of John. Paramount in understanding the views expressed in this book is the recognition that the human spirit is of utmost importance. We can endure many trials and temptations with a good spirit. We can also get along with very little. Happy is the person who looks to and trusts in God—and thereby experiences joy, clarity, a sense of wellbeing, vitality, peace, and contentment. I want all to experience these things; I want each person to know that life is worth living! I want you to gain the benefits of my journey without going through the mud yourselves (as far as that is possible).

Libraries are full of books written by authors who feel a sense of clarity in their quest for happiness and want to share their personal insights for the wellbeing of all. Self-help and pop-psychology books abound, written by well-intentioned people. These have the resemblance of truth, and at their best, offer valid insights, but truth be told, most are little more than the flavor of the month. The question is, do those insights have staying power? Fads come and go. New information reveals flaws and disillusionment. Everyone has an opinion and a perspective. Good intentions do not result in a lived experience. The Bible, on the other hand, was written by the One who formed you in your mother's womb, who knows you better than you do yourself, and who knew you before the foundations of the earth were established. It is general enough to speak to all people yet at the same time, is personal enough to address everyone uniquely. It can be your faithful compass in moments of uncertainty. It is valid because it is divine.

Decades ago, my uncle Norm laughed when he found out that I wanted to write a spiritual book. I was young, inexperienced, even ignorant, and naive, but that is not why he laughed. Though he could have derided me, and he probably had every right to do so, he simply said, "I thought we already had a spiritual book: the Bible!" Since then, I have adopted his view.

I claim no authority other than my own understanding. My intent is to start a respectful conversation, not to impose my opinion upon you. If I have learned anything in my walk with Christ, it is that I am flawed and sometimes shortsighted. I depend on the community to hold me to account and correct me when needed. I ask only that you keep an open mind while hearing me out. Then, we can find points of resonance and disaccord. But for now, just open your Bible to the book of John, and we will delve in. My hope is that by reading this you, too, may share a sense of God's goodness, claim with conviction that life is good and important, and understand that trials are only steppingstones to a closer and deeper life with God!

CHAPTER 1

Jesus As the Authority on Living and Life

Summary: Jesus is the authority on life and living. He knows what each person needs, because he created them. Only he can lead people to the eternal spring of joy and vitality. The Bible is unique in that it is broad enough to reach all people, but specific enough to talk to individual experiences.

Who but the author of life knows what you need to feel life? Who but your creator, who knows you inside and out better than you do yourself, can give thoughtful instruction leading to vitality and peace in ways that you would not recognize. This is grace, that a loving God wants you to be successful in a world of distractions, gave instructions for how to achieve that, and went the whole distance to bring you to the fountain of joy so that you might experience something lasting and sustaining, something eternal.

John begins his story by bringing us to the place of ultimate reality, grounding us in something bigger than ourselves—a story of purpose that supersedes us and points to something magnificently better: the intent and very nature of God himself. "In the beginning" takes us here, back to the first words of Genesis reminding us of the creative and sustaining force that exists eternally. The correlation of "the Word" with Jesus is a clear statement of divinity, underscoring the preexistence of the Triune God who resided in perfect harmony, perfect relationship, from before the dawn of time. This is where the journey starts and where all things are leading, only this time, we are included.

In Genesis God's power is made manifest as the One who causes and creates; it is the force behind everything. In John, "the Word" is associated with this power not only in strength and authority, but as a guiding force seen in the life and teachings of Jesus Christ. The image should instill awe and wonder. Reverence for this power appropriately engenders fear. Fear that restrains and guides is a good thing. God graciously implants this in us for our own wellbeing, to lead us to light. We would not know light had Jesus not come. It is not intuitive to our nature, what with our propensity to self-absorption and the temptations which allure and attract us. But Jesus came to show the way so that life may be in us and our joy may be complete (15: 11), not to end in dissipation or self-gratification, but to become fruitful in love, which attracts people to God. In one sense, John's Gospel is an invitation to participate in God's plan of redemption. Right from the start, it gives purpose and meaning beyond the immediacy of our troubles.

"In Him was life, and that life was the light of [people]" (1: 4). These themes of life and light run throughout the Book of John where light leads to true life. I associate "life" with vitality, or an inner strength which comes from following the "light." It is a remarkable thing that is God-breathed, fulfilling promises made elsewhere. Though "the light shines" in our darkness, we have trouble recognizing it (1: 10).

"The Word became flesh and made his dwelling among us" (1:14). Christianity is not a religion based on the deep thoughts of people. Rather, it is based in the tangible life of a man who turned out to be God. If He is indeed the light, we need to pay attention to His example and teachings; proof that He is the light comes from within. A mature Christian who is filled with the Holy Spirit can feel His presence. This comes from intentionally following the light even when one is not sure why.

Jesus' example and teachings are evident throughout the Bible. "We have seen his glory, the glory of the One and Only, who came from the father, full of grace and truth" (1:14), It is interesting how truth and light revolve around grace. In our religiosity we should ponder this with humility. We should make it the cornerstone of our faith.

How does this look in real time? Jesus made clear that he intended an inner transformation, only accessible through God's grace. God is forming us into loving beings. True, it feels good to love, but can we make ourselves feel love? Can love be more than duty? Jesus makes it clear that if we follow the "light," and discover the "truth" about ourselves and others, and view people with "grace," God will melt our hearts so that we can love like Him (Adapted prophecy from Ezekiel 26: 36; implied throughout John).

Jesus welcomed the outcast, the stranger, the alien, and the marginalized. He loved sinners and offered himself to them. He deferred judgements and spoke tenderly and graciously. He opposed false religion, which is merely external, and offered an alternative. There is a distinction here between the law of Moses and the love of Christ. Religion based solely on rules at the expense of love, omitting grace, is offensive to God.

Jesus graciously bore our faults and infirmities, becoming the perfect sacrifice, providing the necessary work of atonement out of deep love for each of us individually. Keep this in mind. You can never fall so far beyond the pale of God's grace that He will not bring you back! He loves you and your opponent equally. "The Lamb of God," the perfect sacrifice, takes away all our sins. He offers salvation, deliverance, and more, including heaven itself. He offers you a second chance and a better life today, with others, through the Holy Spirit. Learn to heed His call, learn to be disciplined, and make the most of it.

Maybe not unlike you, Nathanael heard this call while sitting beneath a fig tree. In John, this odd exchange between him and Jesus is not given in detail so we can only guess. But something profound happened in the life of this unwitting character. Maybe he was praying for an answer, or a sign. In earnestness he might have opened his heart to God in that preceding moment, "there is nothing false" about him. Whatever the exchange, it is almost comical. To the outside observer one can relate to Jesus in his wry question: "You believe because I told you I saw you under the fig tree?" But Jesus knew Nathanael intimately and completely and welcomed him in, "You shall see greater things than that" (1:45-51).

CHAPTER 2

Saving the Best for Last

God saved his best, most revealing insights through Jesus Christ for last. In the cross, God proclaims his grace and mercy, available to all who chose. In essence, God wants to be known as a gift-giver. This is His expression of love.

The changing of water into wine is really a story about revelation with God leaving "the best for last" (2: 10). Evidently, creation and conscience were not enough to lead us to God. Neither were the miraculous signs of deliverance and the fulfillment of a promise. Not even the law was enough to change our hearts and incline our ears to God almighty. The Bible calls us stiff-necked, obstinate, intent on our own way. We want to be God, directors of our own lives, resistant to sound advice whether it hurts or not. Then Jesus came, calling us to him with an infinite love. He relieves us of our burdens if we will only allow it. He did everything necessary to tear down the dividing wall between us and God. The question is not "am I good enough?" The answer follows the question with an emphatic "no you're not, but God is that good!" The question is not "have I done enough?" The remarkable answer is "Christ has done it all!" It is the only answer to the human dilemma of free will and sin. We cannot do it ourselves. But God can do it in us and through us. It is by his will that we take another breath. And it is by his strength that we can get up, brush ourselves off, and do better. Grace can be transforming. Lifted from the burdens of fear, anger, doubt, and shame, God can instill a spark of love into our lives. Have you not perceived it? You will. And it is a wonderful thing.

In our God-instilled quest for wellbeing, we would do well to take Jesus' mother's advice to those servants: "Do whatever he tells you" (2: 5). In our spiritual blindness we do not always know what is best, so we need to be told. Left to ourselves, we could never find true Christian Joy. But Jesus' light shines in our darkness, and if we would only try first, we might grow into the blessings that Jesus had intended for us from the very dawn of time.

Chapter two moves on to the incident where Jesus clears the temple. In the first century, biographies were not as much chronological as they were thematic, so do not be perplexed or over-concerned about differences in the placing of this story amongst the Gospels. In John it sets up points to be made later as a sort of springboard. Immediately preceding is a claim of revelation with the details yet to be flushed out. John fully intends to elucidate what this revelation is, but first it seems important by way of contrast to illustrate what it is not. It also serves the important purpose of identifying the tension between Jesus and the religious authorities, which escalates throughout the Gospel to the point of crucifixion.

Jesus enters the temple courts and is presumably incensed by mindless routine--religious people doing religious things. Here, it is important to distinguish between religion and relationship. Religion is outward. Adherents of religion participate in anything from abstinence to sacrifice as a sort of proof of devotion, an earning of something that can only be given. It disguises itself in zealous forms often deplete of true contrition or any desire to be changed or transformed.

Sin is hidden in popular culture, in tendencies of self-justification, in self-validating attitudes and learned prejudices, in self-righteousness, and anything else that makes us smugly complacent. Jesus disrupts this atmosphere saying, "Get these out of here! How dare you turn my Father's house into a market!" The problem was not the institution itself, but how it was being observed. A market, buying and selling, a mere exchange was the point of contention. No fear. No true reverence or respect. No commitment to change.

In the book of Matthew, where this story is also recorded, the author has Jesus quoting Isaiah, "My house will be called a house of prayer" Isa. 56:7; Matt. 21: 13 then interjects, "but you are making it a den of robbers." In the previous exchange, were Jesus' opponents robbing God of His right to judge and show grace? John indicates that Jesus knows people's hearts. The human heart is the essence of the matter. And it is in the heart where relationship begins.

In John's story, the Pharisees are appalled by Jesus' angry outburst and ask by whose authority he acts. The answer is a bit of an enigma. For us, twenty-one centuries this side of the resurrection, the meaning is joyously obvious. But for them, it was a further statement of contention. "Destroy this temple, and I will raise it again in three days" (2: 19) spoke blasphemy. Beyond that, it prompted incredulity. They had neither the will nor desire to wait on the miracle. Stuck in their perspectives, they could not accept other possibilities, least of all a miracle.

Nonetheless, the question of Jesus' authority is addressed. John alludes to prophecy (Ps. 16:10), or the miracle of how God can speak of things before they happen. Prophecy exists throughout the Bible pointing to and coming to fulfillment in Jesus Christ. It is one of the marvels of scripture, how people from the past could testify through their experience about a God-given vision that came to fruition in Christ.

John also alludes to "Miraculous signs" (2: 18) as a means by which God validates Jesus' ministry. None other than God himself can so effectively act outside the boundaries of nature as to transform expectations. The proof is in the pudding, so it is said, and Jesus's miracles are wonderous evidence of divine interaction and origin. Seeing a miracle is strong motivation to take heed of Jesus's imploring. Paramount among these in all the Gospels, God marvelously vindicates Jesus' actions, words, and intent by raising him from the dead (after three days)!

Still, above and beyond these, and most relevant to us today, Jesus' authority can be felt from within. Conscience convicts and defines what is good. It affirms and instructs. Led by the Spirit, we are directed to the good. On our own, we are left floundering. But the power of the Holy Spirit leads us upward, confirming at the core of our being that God is good. When we respond, a miracle transpires. Joy and vitality become our strength. Peace allows for patience and endurance. And feelings of wellbeing instill contentment. By God's grace our journey is established, first in the moment, then stretching out to eternity. We have hope which sustains, and a Bible which serves as our map. Jesus' life and teachings are at the center. Illumined by his example we have courage to take the next step.

CHAPTER 3

Born of the Spirit

It is not enough to be baptized by water, but one must be born of the Spirit to obtain life. This is the work of God, a principle that Nicodemus, a religious leader, seemed to have no clue.

The Book of John speaks of two forms of life: inner life and eternal life. Could it be that Nicodemus, a religious teacher, didn't even know about one, much less another? Manmade religion can be burdensome, with its tedious attention to the details of the Law. Rules can be cumbersome if that is all that you see. "For the letter kills, but the spirit gives life" (2 Cor 3: 6b). On this point Jesus is on the side of life. The very author of life, he has the authority to speak about what gives life. Only he can expose the world's empty promises. Only he speaks truth about worldly objects of attraction and to ideas about what the world says can bring a sense of wellbeing; in a sentence, the world's urgent answers and busy proposals are nothing more than tired distractions.

Unaware of this, Nicodemus is shrouded in darkness as he makes his journey to the doorstep of light. In his curiosity he is struck by the validation God gives to Jesus in the workings of "miraculous signs." Jesus immediately confronts him: "I tell you the truth, no one can see the kingdom of God unless he is born again" (3:3). Nicodemus' obtuseness would be humorous if it were not so sad.

So many people throughout history, even Christians, have been bereft of spirit. Today, billions of individuals lack that vigor which presents itself inwardly as vitality. True joy seems elusive, leaving groanings of dissatisfaction brought about by disillusionment. Complaints often begin with the words "they" promised, "they" being the unidentified voices of culture. People try to fill the gap through self-medication: alcohol, drugs, sex, power, popularity, money, work, food, property, etc. It is an endless pursuit of something, emptiness which cannot be filled, anxiety, lack of peace, depression, and inability to thrive amidst the mundane. Truth be told, life is full of quiet moments. How we respond to God in these moments makes all the difference in the world. God wants to give clarity and strength which we can, in turn, offer outwardly. He wants to fill these moments with good things, enduring things, things eternal. And at the heart of it is relationship.

Jesus said in the Sermon on the Mount, "seek first [God's] kingdom and His righteousness, and all these things will be given to you as well" (Matt 6: 33). This is not a prosperity gospel, as some would have it. It is spiritual! Indeed, ultimately it is not what you can get, but what you can give through the overflow of what God has given you: strength, vitality, wellbeing, and peace. Once received, you can accomplish so much. Without it you flounder in your efforts toward the boundaries of numbness or burnout. Insensitive to the things of God, one becomes lost in a sea of mediocrity, left wondering if there is not something better.

So many people have resigned themselves to a life and view of life that is negative. A grim tolerance and a solemn acceptance of this view seem to cloud people's perspectives in a gray haze. Religiously, they are left wondering if there is not something more than these tiresome observances that we follow. Agnostics and atheists say things like, "at least life doesn't suck." And the adage, "life is hard, then you die," is prevalent amongst all. I personally, would not settle on such a view. Led by the Spirit, I believed there was more. Urged onward by God's grace, I found hope in Christ. Like Nicodemus, I needed to be reborn, not of flesh, but of spirit. The Kingdom of God beckoned me with sweet promises of fulfillment.

What, then, is the Kingdom of God? It is nurturing the sick, protecting the vulnerable, binding up the brokenhearted, encouraging the weary, comforting those who mourn, listening to those who are sad, providing for the poor, feeding the hungry, giving respect, learning to love, being a peacemaker, sharing the Gospel. The Kingdom of God exists in every kind action, gracious deed, and work of love. The list goes on and on. There is so much work to do that one should never lack purpose. For everyone, clarity is needed to find one's place. And God gives clarity on a personal level, something that fits one's experiences and demeanors and is as unique as the fingerprints He has given you.

Jesus said in Luke "The kingdom of God does not come with your careful observation, nor will people say, 'Here it is,' or 'There it is,' because the kingdom of God is within you" (17: 20b- 21). You sense it deep down in your soul. It matches you exactly as to understanding and temperament. It is as inquisitive and malleable as your spirit. It loves to learn about self and others. To that end, it gives grace and respect. It thrives on community- giving courage to step out and be useful. It is affirming and loving. It listens without needing to be heard. It comforts and provides. The Kingdom of God and a spiritual birth are inseparable. Yes, like Nicodemus, a spiritual birth is what we need; something which enlivens. For "The Spirit gives life; the flesh counts for nothing" (6:63). This is the first kind of life which John testifies to. The next is eternal.

Jesus alludes to his crucifixion. He then declares God's marvelous intent: "For God so loved the world that he gave his one and only Son, that whoever believes in him shall not perish but have eternal life. For God did not send his Son into the world to condemn the world, but to save the world through him" (3: 16- 17). This assurance is your strength. When assailed by life's tribulations you need something firm to hold on to, something that does not depend on your own success or understanding. Eternal life, the grand destination, the climax, and resting point, lies ahead giving us peace and purpose today. That it is ours as a gift is altogether humbling. Then surely, our humility turns into energy, and our energy instills in us the ability to love.

When we truly examine ourselves, what with our propensity to sin and go astray, and consider the implications of what Christ has accomplished, we stand in wonderous awe. Once on board, the devil will attack you. But these trials will help form you into a more mature Christian with a more robust faith. Afterall, "in all things God works for the good of those who love him" (Rom 8: 28). There will be times when you will doubt. And you will stumble; everyone does. But there's peace for the journey, and God-given vitality for the fight.

Jesus' life and teachings embody this life worth living. Why then do people prefer darkness? Maybe nobody wants to be exposed for what they really are, because this revealing presents itself as a confrontation. Here, change is required. Soul searching and repentance are intrinsic to this arduous task. But people's reluctance is more than laziness. People love the delusion that sin offers. At the root is original sin. Remember, Adam and Eve ate fruit from the tree of knowledge, against God's command, thinking that knowing good and evil would elevate them to God like-status. Today, as then, people want to be gods onto themselves. We want to call the shots. We do not want to be dependent on anyone, not even God. In this, there is a rift in the cosmic scheme, God's intention for harmony in community through dependent living, which free will overrides and takes unlawful advantage of, causing strife and division.

Still, free will is a blessing. There cannot be true love without it, nor could there be genuine worship. This is the dilemma that has plagued the human condition since the dawn of time. The illusion is that we are in control, and that we can somehow taste happiness on our own. Torn from our moorings, we are adrift. We grasp at this and that while we are being carried out to sea. Things look grim. But for those who will listen, for those who can see, Jesus is the lighthouse that will light our way safely home. We are not in control after all. Seeing our condition, a loving God went the full distance, doing for us that which we cannot do for ourselves. Then, lo and behold, we find that grace is transforming. Order is restored when we accept ourselves as created. Life blooms in our hearts, and we find that we can love God and others, maybe for the first time. And it feels good!

John the Baptist was first mentioned in chapter one. Creative license has me waiting until now to discuss him. John, not the author of this book, was a splendid example of the old order which was under the Law and Prophets. He, like few others, recognized that the Law and the Prophets were only intended to point to someone or something. And it was mysteriously revealed to him that Jesus was that to which they pointed, a new order.

Jesus says of John, "Truly I tell you, among those born of women there has not risen anyone greater than John the Baptist; yet whoever is least in the kingdom of heaven is greater than he" (Matt 11: 11). The old order tended to instill pride and feelings of self-reliance, while the new order freely submits to God. The old order was stern and hardhearted; the new order is gracious and kind, creating room in our hearts for feelings of love. The old order was legalistic, while the new order promotes a free exchange with God and others, resulting in harmony and a tender touch. The old order is sometimes construed as unforgiving, while the new order is full of grace and truth. Christ sees members of the new order as great because they willingly see themselves as least. The burden of responsibility has been lifted, and we are free, free to truly live.

In pointing to Jesus, John realizes that "(Jesus) must become greater; I must become less" (3: 30). This is true of all Christians. It is a wonderful day, filled with joy, when one gladly relinquishes the reins of their lives to Christ. We become smaller and smaller as Christ works His power in us. As mother Teresa once indicated, we do no great things here, we do little things with great love. That is the essence. We are the beneficiaries. God enlivens our spirits giving us strength. He directs our paths. He works in us and through us as instruments of His good purpose. He is the carpenter; we are the tools. When we follow Jesus' truth, we find it valid because it is confirmed in our spirits. All of this is to God's glory!

CHAPTER 4

Living Water

Christ offers living water to all who thirst. This living water is spiritual. It presents itself as joy, vitality, peace, wellbeing, and strength.

Jesus and his disciples travel through Samaria enroute back to Galilee. Tired from the journey, they stop at Sychar "near the plot of ground Jacob had given to his son Joseph" (4: 5). There was a well there, known as Jacob's well, where Jesus encountered a Samaritan woman who had come from town to draw water.

The incident is remarkable in that Jews did not associate with Samaritans because of prejudices about ethnic origins. There were also religious divisions, and Jewish men did not typically associate with women who were strangers. Here, in John 4, Jesus breaks down multiple barriers all at the same time. This speaks volumes about Jesus' heart and ministry. This sets a course that we would do well to pay attention to and follow earnestly in our lives today.

His disciples went into town to buy food, leaving Jesus alone. Jesus takes this opportunity to initiate conversation. He asks the Samaritan woman for a drink. The woman is astonished. Tenderly, Jesus continues, "If you knew the gift of God and who it is that asks you for a drink, you would have asked Him, and he would have given you living water" (4: 10). The woman takes him literally and reveals doubts of her own. Jesus answers, "Everyone who drinks this water will be thirsty again, but whoever drinks the water I give him will never thirst. Indeed, the water I give him will become in him a spring of water welling up to eternal life" (4: 13- 14).

The implications are remarkable. What Jesus gives is immediate and lasting. We all thirst for a sense of wellbeing in our dry and weary lives. We all yearn for something satisfying, something eternal which will enliven our spirits and give us hope. We want to do good. We want to be involved in something meaningful. Jesus gives hope by showing the way.

One can go a long way with a healthy spirit. One can overcome obstacles while maintaining a positive outlook. One can thrive where others barely survive. Seeing clearly, one can resist temptation and make healthy choices; choices which enrich our lives and lead to the fruition of

God's promises. A journey taken with joy and vitality is a wonderful thing.

Some people call what I am talking about "realized eschatology," and in a sense it is. Being born of the spirit instills joy and energy which wells up to eternity. The more mature one becomes in their faith, the more persistent the experience is. New life starts today in this world, which carries forward into heaven. Sure, there will be trials. And one will feel sad or angry at appropriate moments. But feelings of love for God and others will endure. And you will have what it takes to comfort and inspire others, even in times of trouble.

The metaphor eludes her, so Jesus' next step is to reveal her life to her. She must have been embarrassed to have had so many husbands. And who knows what other details there might have been causing her to cringe. In our lives, a part of the Holy Spirit's work is to convict us. We must recognize and feel where we have been, then want change, before God will work in us. Ultimately, God breathes transformation into desperate situations. Understanding where and why we have strayed is the first step. God initiates, we respond.

The matter of where one worships is important. Jesus informs her that it is neither on what turned out to be Mount Gerizim, nor even in Jerusalem, that matters. True worship is from the heart and can be done everywhere. Prominently, worship is what we do day to day, shown in our actions as we seek the kingdom of God. Yet, it is also how we feel. A spirit of joy that praises God with thanksgiving is an offering to God "in spirit and truth" (4: 23). When we view God's beautiful creation with unsurpassed awe and appreciation, that is worshiping in spirit and truth. When we are moved by the cross of Christ to the point of tears and are filled with humility and gratitude, that is worshiping in spirit and truth. Someone once told me that God is most pleased with us when we are most pleased with Him. True worship comes from the core of our being when we feel lifted and exuberant.

The disciples return with food. They urge Jesus to eat. Meanwhile, the woman had run back to town to bear witness about her experience. As to food, Jesus informs his disciples that his food, which they still knew nothing about, is to do God's will right up to completion. His food is to work for the Kingdom of God, resulting in a new experience, a new life, which he brings, even as he speaks.

Consider this new life, and the realignment implied in Jesus' temptation recorded in Matthew 4. After forty days in the desert without food, he surely was hungry. The devil urged him to prove himself by turning rock into bread. He could have but did not. Citing scripture he said, "Man does not live on bread alone, but on every word that comes from the mouth of God" (4: 4). This is a resounding acknowledgement affirming that we are all spiritual beings first. Spirit is more important than body. And if Jesus found nourishment in doing God's will, we should follow his lead and find satisfaction in doing his will!

The harvest is ripe. People are yearning to be made right, to feel a sense of wellbeing. So, join in! Find your place to partake and be filled. Find the place where God pours life into you to the point of overflowing and be fruitful. Afterall, our ministries are initiated and sustained by this abundant spring welling up from inside. We cannot do it on our own. Without Jesus, we cannot even see clearly enough to try. It is God testing and proving his perfect will for our lives to the end that we might know and experience what is pleasing to him, and what is ultimately good for the Kingdom of Heaven (Romans 12: 2), and good for us too.

Jesus stayed with the Samaritans for two days, "And because of his words many more became believers" (4: 41). He then continued to Galilee where he was confronted by a "certain royal official whose son lay sick at Capernaum" (4: 46). The man begged Jesus to come and heal his son who was close to death. Exhausted, Jesus answered, "Unless you people see miraculous signs and wonders you will never believe," as if he mourned over unbelief. We are like the official, needing to experience results before we believe. And Jesus compassionately acquiesces. From the vantage point of a person whose life circumstances have taken him far from God, a miracle is needed. We feel beleaguered and brutalized, much in need of healing.

At this point God could have been aloof, saying I told you so, or you get what you deserve. But that is not in God's nature. Instead, He sent his Son to bind our wounds. As Isaiah confirms: "He was wounded for our transgressions, he was bruised for our iniquities: the chastisement of our peace was upon him; and with his stripes we are healed" (Isaiah 53: 5). In this story, Jesus heals the son and many more believed.

CHAPTER 5

A Healing and a Warning

Jesus heals a man, and gives fair warning: "Stop sinning or something worse may happen to you." Continued obstinance invites suffering. I am reminded of the spirit who was cast out only to return with seven demons worse than he finding the place swept out and clean. Jesus insists that the second condition is worse than the first.

Jesus heals a paralytic. Due to John's careful economy of words, I cannot tell the story any more succinctly. I will mention, though, Jesus' compassionate attitude toward the recipient of the miracle: "Do you want to get well?" (5: 6). Jesus approaches all of us the same way. In our misery, He comes to offer a better life. Only he has the power to heal. Miraculously, he knows everything about our condition: our experiences, weaknesses, settled attitudes, and desires. Jesus wishes to transform us, to offer light to penetrate the darkness of a seemingly hopeless situation. The question is, will we allow beneficial, positive change?

In the story, the paralytic's desperation overcomes his resistance. And he is healed! In the telling of this incredible act of mercy, the story not only reveals the motives behind the increased tension between Jesus and the religious leaders, moving the coming persecution forward as an important dimension to John's plot, but it also underscores Jesus' remarkable power to invade the circumstances of this tired and weary world, bringing about meaningful and tangible relief. We too cry out for help. We too are desperate for deliverance. Conditions are ripe for a harvest of renewal.

Once healed, what do we do next? Afterall, we still have an entire life ahead of us. With a desire to give us everything we need to succeed, Jesus offers fair warning: "Stop sinning or something worse may happen to you" (5: 14). I am reminded of Jesus' relevant words in Matthew 12: 43- 45: "When an impure spirit comes out of a person, it goes through arid places seeking rest and does not find it. Then it says, 'I will return to the house I left.' When it arrives, it finds the house unoccupied, swept clean and put in order. Then it goes and takes with it seven other spirits more wicked than itself, and they go in and live there. And the final condition of that person is worse than the first."

Can things get worse? Can we feel even worse than we do today? The Bible affirms that "The fear of the Lord is the beginning of wisdom" (Proverbs 9: 10). It is not all of wisdom, but it is its start. When we fear the Lord, we acknowledge our awareness of consequences. Fear is appropriate. It bridles our temperaments and attitudes and keeps us safe from our own impulses.

Jesus gives new life. He says, "pick up your mat and walk." This is not so much about heaven as it is about living the remainder of our days here on earth. In this time, we can choose joy or be miserable throughout the duration. So, we have meaningful choices to make here on earth, choices that effect our wellbeing and fruitfulness. Do we continue to be settled in our sin? Or do we heed God's call and allow Him to transform us? If we choose unwisely, it is not that God will actively seek us out in retribution. But He will allow us to reap what we've sown. In Romans, while describing a people bent on having their own way, it is repeated three times that God "gave them over" to the consequences of following their own path (1: 24-28). In my journey, God was talking to me clearly about sobriety. I resisted for the longest time while wallowing in self-imposed pain; I was making no headway. Then I listened, and God started blessing me with a healthy spirit. I had energy to serve, staying power, clarity, and a joy-filled heart.

Now, to an alcoholic, the temptation remains every day. And each day I pray for strength. I do not want to return to unfruitfulness and the angst associated with the penalty of sin. By now I understand that to sin is to invite doubt. And doubt is a terrible burden to bear. It seeps into every aspect of life and leaves us exposed. Gone is security. Gone is peace. Gone is vitality and strength. Today, when temptation is strong, I remember the words of Isaiah 42:

> You have seen many things, but you pay no attention; your ears are open, but you do not listen. It pleased the LORD for the sake of his righteousness to make his law great and glorious. But this is a people plundered and looted, all of them trapped in pits or hidden away in prisons. They have become plunder, with no one to rescue them; they have been made loot, with no one to say, "Send them back." Which of you will listen to this or pay close attention in time to come? Who handed Jacob over to become loot, and Israel to the plunderers? Was it not the LORD, against whom we have sinned? For they would not follow his ways; they did not obey his law. So he poured out on them his burning anger, the violence of war. It enveloped them in flames, yet they did not understand; it consumed them, but they did not take it to heart (20-25).

In me, God gave hearing to a deaf man, and sight to one who was blind. I am now resolute. I take these things to heart. That is not to say that I am perfect. All people have blind spots, and I am sure that others can readily pick out many of my blemishes. But I listen to what God is talking to me about--sobriety! This is not about us getting our legalistic ducks in a row to prepare ourselves for blessings. It is about listening to the Holy Spirit, and not grieving Him with flagrant offences. For you, if you have the Holy Spirit, God is talking to you, and the thing that He is talking to you about is fundamental and personal to you! He knows your weaknesses and potential. He knows how sin affects you. When you first hear, you might recoil and remain obstinate, a recipe for disaster. You will be miserable in your efforts to be distracted. Not till you surrender will you feel peace and vitality and joy. It is about learning a lesson particular to you. And God will reveal himself and give clarity to you in ways that only you can understand.

Once on board, you will feel great. And the more mature you are in your faith the more sustaining that feeling will be. But watch out for pride. The statement "I feel great" might turn into the perception that "I am great," and the fall which that engenders is painful. Also, after feeling good about yourself for a time the temptation might arise in you to say, "would it really hurt to backslide just a bit?" For me, the temptation to drink is always there, but I fear that even one drink will impel me downward, and I will lose all the ground that I have gained. Each step precedes the next. And it is a bit of a mystery how chosen courses will determine how one feels and thinks the next day or week, and what one will experience tomorrow.

One promise that God makes is found in Proverbs 3: 5- 8: "Trust in the Lord with all your heart and lean not on your own understanding; in all your ways acknowledge him, and he will make your paths straight. Do not be wise in your own eyes; fear the Lord and shun evil. This will bring health to your body and nourishment to your bones." Come what may, I want to be confident that God is directing my paths. Only then can I stand firm and patiently wait on the Lord.

Sadly, there are so many people who cannot handle joy. They are either not disciplined enough, or they obstinately choose their own path. Strangely, there is not free will without two or more tenable choices. We live in a world where there are more choices than we know what to do with. And everyone is telling you something different about what you need. Have an anchor, Jesus Christ. Have a resource, the Bible. Only then are you truly free to live a life worth living. This is life through the Son who "gives life to whom he is pleased to give it" (5: 21).

To see Jesus at work in you, and in this world, is to see God the Father. And by honoring Jesus through our behavior, we are honoring God the Father and have already crossed over from death to life (5: 24). For those who have the Holy Spirit, heaven is assured. And for those who have the Holy Spirit, judgement is administered in this world alone. Here, there is a strange paradox in that by seeking to please Jesus we end up benefiting ourselves. For everything that God asks of us is really for our own good. First seek the kingdom of God, and all else will fall in place.

You might ask by what testimony can I trust it is true. John, chapter five, lists four relevant ones. First, John the Baptist harkens from the old order. He was a lamp-giving light for a while (5: 35). Then the signs and wonders, or the miracles performed by Christ are God's validations of Jesus' ministry. Thirdly, all prophecy from the Old Testament point convincingly to Jesus. And fourthly, as a predecessor to all prophecy, Moses himself pointed unabashedly to Christ Jesus our Lord; the rejection of said prophesy resulting in confusion about the Law. Notwithstanding, a fifth testimony, not mentioned here, comes from within. This is potentially the most convincing of all testimonies because it is immediately tangible. Stated plainly, following Jesus instills a sense of wellbeing. Whether this is experienced as peace, joy, vitality, or strength-giving clarity is beside the point. Regardless of circumstance, whether good or bad, easy, or hard, exuberant, or lamentable, life is the result. This life helps you encourage the downhearted in troubled times, to seek justice, to comfort mourners even in their deepest grief, to build someone up who is feeling down, to offer peace as a suitable outcome, to endure hate or rejection, or respond positively to any other situation. The list goes on. Concerning the how, Jesus gives light. Concerning the why, following Jesus gives life to the soul.

CHAPTER 6

Jesus As the Bread of Life

Jesus is the bread of life. This bread is doing his will. It sustains.

I believe that Jesus truly fed five thousand with meager resources. But that does not take away from the value of the implied metaphor. On one level, it is a story about God's miraculous provision. At the same time, it is a story about finding satisfaction in living out what Jesus taught and represented in his earthly life.

Upon seeing this miraculous sign, the people wanted to seize Jesus and make him king. But Jesus withdrew to a place of solitude. The disciples got into a boat and pushed off, intending to reach the distant shore at Capernaum. The wind increased and the seas got rough. They feared for their lives like we do when situations seem untenable; believing in Christ does not ensure that we will not experience rocky waters. Responding to their struggle, Jesus approached; the disciples perceived him to be walking on water. The men were terrified. Jesus reassures them and tells them not to fear. Upon taking Jesus into the boat, the storm subsided, and the disciples found themselves safely at their destination.

If the rocky waters represent chaos, then Jesus represents safety. This is relevant to us today. Think about it; there are billions of people in the world, all with their own agendas, some imposing their will by force. Selfishness abounds with few people keeping their eyes on the needs of community. In this treacherous bustle, the devil wants to distract us from God's assurances. He implores, "look out for number one, just take care of yourself." We yearn for safety, often not looking to the God who has revealed himself time and time again as the deliverer. Jesus is the solid ground, the firm footing, the rock on which we stand.

Remember, "Acknowledge God in all your ways and he will direct your paths" (Proverbs 3: 6). According to John, acknowledging God has everything to do with love for neighbor. Amidst this chaos, this one thing is critical: how do we love? The Sermon on the mount is a picture of love, as is 1 Corinthians chapter 13. But it is not enough to have a picture which can be imposed legalistically. We need inner transformation, God working in us to grow us in love.

True worship is not as much about physical deeds as it is about growing to the point where one feels love for all people. The responding deeds are then inevitable. Getting there can be a lifelong process, a purpose which keeps us from settling into dissipation, bitterness, irritation, grumpiness, and discontentment. Some people have been so hurt that they separate themselves from people. This is a big mistake. God formed us as relational beings and we are best off when we embrace and respect each other.

This is an important message because with people as they are, conflict is inevitable. How we respond is of the utmost importance. With Christ, we can approach situations with grace, tenderness, gentleness, kindness, and compassion. We can be a fragrant offering that attracts people to Jesus' way.

At this point in John's story, we are about to see resistance. Previously, being benefactors of Jesus' miracles caused enthusiasm to the point where they wanted to make him king. Now they hear a hard message which causes people to fall away.

"The work of God is this: to believe in the one he has sent" (6: 29). Belief here means trusting Jesus to the point of obedience. Only after trying, will you taste that the Lord is truly good and be encouraged. Only after trying, will you find conviction that Christ's way is best and that his instruction is relevant and meaningful to you today.

Jesus had already explained that his food was to do the Father's will. Similarly, our food is eating the bread which Jesus provides, his flesh, which is essentially doing his will. In John, there was much controversy about what this might mean. In their dullness, people did not grasp the metaphor and turned away. Today, there have been many words spent in explaining different possibilities.

People are inclined to make things more difficult than they need to be. One thing is for certain in this difficult saying; following Christ requires commitment. You must be persistent to discover that in Jesus, there is life, and that whoever comes will never go hungry, and that whoever believes will never be thirsty (6: 35). It is a metaphor about true life and where it comes from. Commitment is obligatory, a message that turns many away today.

Who wants to sacrifice? Who wants to be obedient and disciplined? Who wants to be the least? Who wants to serve? These principles are not intuitive. Had God not revealed them we would still be left floundering at sea. But God guides us and encourages us to be persistent, and low and behold, with time and effort, we discover a life worth living!

God is forming you in your trials. God is drawing you right now with the message of relief and deliverance. We all yearn for a day when our ship comes in and we feel a sense of wholeness. The reward is out there, identified in this section of John with the persistent language about eternal life. It is somewhere in the distant future which drives us onward. God instills in us that hope. It keeps us alive and moving forward. But the good news of what Jesus is all about is that we do not have to wait. We can experience wholeness, wellbeing, even vitality right now, eternal springs welling up from inside--at last, deliverance.

Many people do not try. The insistence on commitment, effort, and obligation is repelling, and to some bent on their theology, or mere ideas, it is offensive. But remember, we are not talking about heaven, but true life today. Some people get frustrated by failures brought about by insincere gestures and give up. Some people are not persistent. Though they have the will to live, they resist transformation. At this point Jesus asks the twelve, "You do not want to leave too, do you?" Peter speaks for all who are hungry, for all who thirst, "Lord, to whom shall we go? You have the words of eternal life" (6: 67-68).

Some people are distracted by an undercurrent throughout this chapter and make it the whole thing. Murmurings of predestination crop up enticing a few who imagine that they are on the right side. Often, their views only serve to rationalize themselves. But the fact is that the doctrine of predestination is a mystery that we, in our finite awareness, cannot fully appreciate. We can only stand in awe at a God who is omniscient and omnipotent. And we must consider the fact that because he knows the outcome does not mean he directs all things. There seems to be a certain randomness about life. Afterall, does not the freedom for individuals to choose good or bad make our experience dependent on them? We are not robots. The command to choose implies a potential variable in outcomes. Yes, God takes every opportunity to turn bad into good. And ultimately, he is in control. But we are not to make him out as a hard God who takes out what he does not put in and reaps what he did not sow (Luke 19: 11-27).

The truth of the matter is that we experience God as a free will proposition. All the imperatives of the Bible scream free will. So, that is how we must approach God, as a choice or opportunity. I personally am settled in this mystery by considering the words of one of my pastors. He said that on the gates of heaven there is a sign overhead that exclaims "everyone is welcome" as one enters. Then passing through and looking back one finds the words "chosen from before the dawn of time." The mystery should instill humility, not pride. The good news is that God is sowing seeds in you right now. Choose wisely.

CHAPTER 7

Try and See!

Jesus invites us to try and see to find out if he speaks on his own or if his instruction is from God. Our spiritual wellness is the litmus test.

The tension between Jesus and his opponents had risen to the point where they wanted to take his life (7: 1). They were incensed, not only because he performed miracles on the Sabbath, which supposedly broke the law, but he was even putting himself on equal terms with God. Many admitted that Jesus spoke with authority, and that his miracles could not happen apart from God. Still, at the Feast of Tabernacles there were conflicting whisperings about him. Some said that he was a good man, while others said that he deceives the people (7: 12). In answer, Jesus gives a clear challenge: "If anyone chooses to do God's will, he will find out whether my teaching comes from God or whether I speak on my own" (7: 17). Is this a challenge or an invitation? Plain words, "try it and see!"

Is Jesus demon-possessed, or is he the Christ? Should they seize him, or should they bow down and put their faith in him? Confusion, a guard arrives, a cryptic saying, and a surprising testimony ensue. Then, on the last day of the feast, "Jesus stood and said in a loud voice, if anyone is thirsty, let him come to me and drink. Whoever believes in me, as the Scripture has said, streams of living water will flow from within him" (7: 37-38). Back then, the religious leaders and Pharisees and scribes were doubtful. And they might have wondered about the man who made this claim. But today, twenty-one hundred years this side of the resurrection, many can attest to the life-giving power of the Spirit of God.

It makes you wonder about those religious leaders and Pharisees and scribes: how could they be so blind? In 2 Timothy, the apostle Paul gives a piercing reproach to such people saying that they are "always learning but never able to come to a knowledge of the truth" (3: 7). Today, we have the same problem. People reading and going to Bible study, people going to church, and people listening to Christian radio, but never coming to the point of serious application which would teach them what they cannot quite comprehend apart from doing the true works of God. Suffering in their good intentions, they miss the point and reject nourishment. Instead of feeling joy and love, they wallow in bitterness and irritation. Instead of being transformed by grace, they remain resolute in their hard heartedness.

For the religious leaders and Pharisees and scribes in Jesus' day, the problem also was not a lack of zeal. "For I can testify about them that they are zealous for God, but their zeal is not based on knowledge" (Romans 10: 2). They revered the law, making it an idol instead of a teacher at the expense of love. They honored the law over people, making them judgmental and proud. Like some people today, they were an obstacle standing in the way of people yearning to get to God, not a fragrant offering that attracts. They were harsh and cold and pushed people out.

Jesus, on the other hand, welcomes sinners and outcasts. He affirms the marginalized. He tends to people's needs. He mourns over people who struggle. He offers a way to health and wellbeing. He is God's healing answer to the human dilemma of pain and suffering.

The religion of the religious leaders and Pharisees and scribes had the "form of godliness but denied its power" (2 Timothy 3: 5). Their religion was meant to control behavior, not transform lives. As to transformation, that is the power of God through Christ Jesus our Lord. It comes from a paradigm shift, a change in perspective, which begins by a renewal of the mind (Romans 12: 2). As to power, God infuses energy into people who are aligned with him. It is not a matter of outer ceremony, which can be shallow and selfish. Isaiah spoke on this very point: "To what purpose is the multitude of your sacrifices to me? I have had enough of burnt offerings of rams and the fat of fed cattle. I do not delight in the blood of bulls, or of lambs or goats. When you come to appear before me, who has required this from your hand, to trample my courts" (1: 11-12)? God wants, and supports, inner change. "Learn to do good; seek justice, rebuke the oppressor, defend the fatherless, plead for the widow" (1: 17). Merely sitting in a pew does not accomplish anything, unless an appreciation for the story of God's redeeming love demonstrated on the cross of Christ melts your hard heart to the point of action. Grace engenders humility, which leads to peace, which buds into love, which is experienced as joy and wellbeing, which sustains us in our efforts to be fruitful for God. These Jews were not open to this.

Still, Jesus beckons, "Come to me, all you who are weary and burdened, and I will give you rest. Take my yoke upon you and learn from me, for I am gentle and humble in heart, and you will find rest for your souls. For my yoke is easy and my burden is light" (Matthew 11: 28-30).

Your brokenness is staring you right in the face. It keeps you up at night and invades your quiet moments. Sometimes it even manifests itself in bad decisions. Do not ignore it by busying yourself with worldly distractions. With God's help, do something about it. If you are actively engaged with God, He is talking to you. Figure out what

He is talking to you about and work on that. Hone it down to two or three things and pray for help. Commit yourself to learning and following His will for your life.

Maybe it is just one thing. Figure it out and submit! Know in your efforts that Jesus' yoke is easy, not effortless, but well suited, as in exactly fitted to your personality and circumstance. He knows everything about you. He can give you clarity about your life. He understands and loves you as an individual! His words are relevant to your needs. This is not about heaven. It is about your life today! It is about your spirit. So, what are you going to do. Here in John's gospel God is imploring you to obey to the end that you might understand, that you might taste and see that the Lord is good. Aren't you curious where it might lead?

Nicodemus was interested and was making slow progress. We find him, once again, here at the end of this chapter defending Jesus in front of the opposition.

CHAPTER 8

The Truth Will Set You Free

Only when we are led by the Spirit and receive clarity through discipline are we truly free in a world of bondage.

Jesus encounters a woman who reportedly was caught in adultery. It does not matter to me that this story is not found in the earliest manuscripts, because it fits well with everything I have read or heard about Jesus Christ. It is consistent. And the themes that it engenders move seamlessly forward, especially in the motives of the accusers. The motives, which advance the tension between Jesus and his opponents, though, are not as important as the message.

It is a story about self-examination. We realize that we all have flaws and regrets; we should not judge. The idiom, "there but for the grace of God go I" applies. We are all capable of the same mistakes given similar circumstances. Our response to other's situations should be filled with humility and grace. Jesus' words to the woman after all her accusers withdraw, though a bit more pointed, basically advise her to learn from her mistakes. We can all take that to heart as we move forward in life. Grace is transforming, relieving us of emotions that cripple and bind us. But grace is not an excuse for further misdeeds.

Life is full of choices. Negotiating these, we look to Jesus who is himself a light to our path. This light ensures that we will not walk in harmful darkness. Following the direction of this light ultimately leads to LIFE!

Maybe referring to the example of the accusers, Jesus testifies that people judge by human standards, or what we can see from the outside. God, on the other hand, judges the heart, and his judgements are right. Not only that, but God's judgements are intended to be transformational. God and Jesus are one. Following Jesus brings life. Rejecting Jesus brings death, spiritual death for sure.

A metaphorical prophecy about Jesus' coming death ensues. This is important, for we will learn that foundational truth, which is the impetus behind all of our best efforts, including our wellbeing, is held together by the cross. It starts with promises about those things which are most important, eternity. It leads to a conviction about who we are and where we have been, and the realization that we are helpless. It promises purpose and the hope of something better. The prophecy includes an appreciation for everyone, for since the time of Adam we have all struggled with the same basic flaws. Nothing has changed except for redemption through grace, and the power of the Holy Spirit to change lives. An invitation is proclaimed from the outstretched arms of Jesus on a cross. Here, grace and judgement kiss. Here, the tensions of the world are resolved.

Verse 31 tells us that holding to Jesus' teachings proves love and commitment to God. This is the required condition for true life to unfold. Pre-Christ, we are slaves to the forces of this world. Post-resurrection, we are free to please God. This results from persistence to the principles of the kingdom of heaven.

At first it dawns on us like the morning sun. Maybe for the first time we see our choices clearly. Maybe for the first time we recognize our obstacles for what they truly are. Previously, we were slaves to our own unhealthy desires, having been pulled along by the current of culture, not asking questions, but simply going with the flow. Then, we could not even see the matters of importance. We were spiritually blind.

As we progress, God's light shines more radiantly. As we acknowledge that there is good and bad in the world, which presents itself as an inscrutable mystery, we can begin to see the importance of choosing God and life. Suddenly, we see the good and bad without feelings of compulsion. As Jesus said, "If you hold to my teachings, you are really my disciples. Then you will know the truth, and the truth will set you free" (8: 31-32).

Today, we can joyfully make a choice for God. Our hearts sing as we step in his direction. Then we run with a sense of wellbeing and thankfulness. God has pulled us out of the pit. And we praise him in his infinite goodness.

Maybe this is what God wanted all along, for us to make a free choice. The whole world is imbued with his goodness. Creation sings of his glory. Full of gratitude, our spirits freely testify to the God of love. We cannot get there on our own; we never could. But he offers it, first on the cross, then through the Holy Spirit. God made a way bringing us to a point of true freedom, a moment of decision; let us make good choices.

Unimaginable as it may seem, the religious leaders and Pharisees and scribes reject Jesus' invitation; some people just argue for the sake of argument. Settled in their learned perspectives, clinging to them in unmalleable persistence, wanting nothing other than to be justified in their thinking, they reject the very source of life. People do not want to unlearn things or admit that they are wrong. Instead, we deflect, and finger point with stiff-necked incredulity. What we do not want to do is take our medicine, a dose of humility, which tastes bad but brings healing. If you are proud, stubborn, spiteful to the point of cutting off your own nose to prove a point to your face, just take your medicine. It is better for the long run, and you will, in time, find happiness and see its benefit. Be open to another perspective. Be circumspect and listen to instruction keeping in mind that it is God who is the potter, and we are just the clay. God, in his infinite wisdom, will form us into something wonderful and useful. Trust that and know that keeping Jesus' words is the antidote to spiritual death.

The chapter ends with a clear statement of Christ's divinity. He is the eternal word. He speaks with authority as the holder and giver of life. "Abraham rejoiced at the thought of seeing (Jesus') day" (8: 56). In fact, all the prophets looked ahead to a time when God would reign in people's hearts. For freedom we have been called, real freedom! So, let freedom reign in your heart, and heed God's call.

CHAPTER 9

Spiritual Blindness

Spiritual blindness is a real problem. It prevents us from seeing clearly, which affects our behavior. Jesus breaks the cycle of despair by offering true light.

Not all tragedy and suffering are caused by sin. It is essential to grasp this important point before ministering to people. Luke 13: 1-5 repeats this message. The story of Job exclaims this message. And Jesus says it here at an important point in John (9: 3). Sometimes trouble exists for the sole purpose of glorifying God. This is not to say that God tempts us by causing suffering, or that all tragedy is his doing. Afterall, at some level, God allows the world to run its course causing what appears to be random chance; that is how we experience it anyway. It is not necessary for us to understand this mystery; just proceed with a sense of awe and humility. And know that God can work good into all situations, and he is pleased to deliver you if you are willing.

Again, we have a real-life story that also serves as a metaphor: God gives sight to the blind. For the man who was born blind, the healing happens on the Sabbath, and, inexplicably, this point overshadows the marvel of what had just happened. Unbelief ensues, along with a profusion of questions in a court-like setting. For the Pharisees, they could only see what they wanted to see, a pre-condition of spiritual blindness.

The Pharisees prove, and we continue to affirm, that understanding spiritual blindness is an elusive task. Our learned presuppositions and expectations get in the way. In fear, we reject anything new. We protect the bricks at the base of our walls of reality thinking that if these are removed, our very sense of being would collapse. We guard against the slippery slope. We lash out in defense. But truth and light await, unavoidable to the heart that seeks personal wholeness and communal peace. God restores harmony. He appears like dew on the thirsty cactus. He creates streams of living water in the desert of our existence.

Spiritual blindness shrouds us when all that we can see is our pain. It pervades us completely when we fear. It confuses us when we doubt. Spiritual blindness overwhelms us when we are paralyzed by shame. Its ally is pride. Its nemesis is love.

Spiritual blindness also leads us astray when we are enamored by the distractions that this world offers, taking us away from the things that really matter. It can be situational, but more often, it is a persistent condition. Prejudice, hate, and judgement come from it. Grace, affirmation, and appreciation, on the other hand, come from light.

Spiritual blindness causes feelings of emptiness, despair, anger, and sorrow. Light is revealed in feelings of joy, vitality, wellbeing, peace, and a sense of purpose. This world's promises might have the appearance of light, but they inevitably lead to disillusionment, frustration, and disappointment. Light is lasting and eternally satisfying. Distinguishing between the two is important.

The Bible warns that the heart is deceptive (Jeremiah 17: 9). It can lead us astray. Only the light and life that Jesus brings is salubrious and sustainable. In the end, the proof is obvious and true. Light produces growth. So, when your heart rejoices in appreciation to a God who has proven himself good, that comes from light. When your heart sings at the words and deeds of Jesus, and you are inspired in a moment of clarity, that comes from light.

Others might add what I leave out. That is alright. Just know up front that everyone is susceptible to spiritual blindness; there are no human experts. Sin causes doubt and confusion, which is a predetermined term of our existence here on earth. God chose this as a tool used to form us into mature Christians. Do not grieve the spirit and give God a reason to withdraw. This ultimately leads to suffering.. Heed Jesus' call. Only he can speak rightly about the subject at hand. Love is the goal, not out of duty, but feelings of affection that unite us in solidarity to each other.

Be warned about the devil who distracts and lies. It is his desire to keep you off balance. If you have the Holy Spirit he cannot take heaven from you, but he can disrupt your fruitfulness. At one moment you might find yourself basking in light. He will take the opportunity to encourage you to take this beyond its limits to the point of trouble. Aware of this you choose another course. He is right behind beckoning further. Christ keeps you focused; keep your eyes firmly on him. Follow his words and deeds. His way is the middle ground between the legalists and libertines, the narrow path which leads to light.

Jesus leaves us here with a cryptic saying. Here is the acknowledgement that if God had not revealed himself in Christ, our floundering would not be held against us. But Christ did come to offer direction. For those who refuse the light and life which he offers, for those too stubborn to acknowledge truth, for those who have weighed the difference and claim that they see something better, there is only judgement left and the resulting downward spiral.

CHAPTER 10

Jesus As the Good Shepherd

Jesus is the good shepherd who goes on ahead and leads by example. He leads us to green pastures. He cares.

Chapter 10 falls right on the heels of the discussion about spiritual blindness. Here, we have comparisons between true religion where Christ is the shepherd, and false religions where leaders are presented as thieves and robbers. Jesus is the shepherd who enters the sheep's pen by the gate. The sheep recognize him by his voice. This might be an allusion to the work of the Holy Spirit. Believers learn to hear and respond to God's familiar call. It is a relationship of trust.

The shepherd knows his sheep and calls them by name, which is a very personal image. Once safely under his care, the sheep follow. Note, Jesus goes on ahead because he does not expect the sheep to tread on ground that he has not already investigated. In God's grand scheme of salvation, Jesus takes on humanity and charts the terrain. In his baptism he claims solidarity with people and goes on ahead.

To clarify, Jesus says it again in slightly different words. Here, Jesus is the gate. All who came before, who taught works-based religion, were thieves and robbers. They came only to steal, kill, and destroy. In Matthew 23, we have a depiction of leaders who adhere to such religions, with a scalding condemnation directed at them: "They tie up heavy, cumbersome loads and put them on other people's shoulders, but they themselves are not willing to lift a finger to move them. Everything they do is done for people to see... [they] shut the door of the kingdom of heaven in people's faces. [They themselves] do not enter, nor will ([they] let those enter who are trying to. [They] travel over land and sea to win a single convert, and when [they] have succeeded, [they] make them twice as much a child of hell as [they] are" (4-5a, 13-14). In a few words, they are proud, self-righteous hypocrites, and are judgmental. They are not merciful. They have no grace.

Jesus, on the other hand, provides safe pasture, leads beside still waters, and restores the soul (Psalm 23). He came so that we may have life and have it to the full (10: 10b). As proof he laid down his life as a ransom for all. In him is the gift of salvation for all who believe. It is free! Such news has the potential for inner transformation. Religion is no longer drudgery, a task to perform, or an obligation to meet. We no longer must climb that mountain. The legalists take away our joy. But Christ restores peace, promises eternal life in heaven, and offers true life right now in the land of the living. God tore down the curtain from top to bottom, meaning it is his work from start to finish. As the Alpha and Omega, he demolished the dividing wall, making himself available anytime in prayer.

At these words the crowd was divided. Some thought him to be a heretic, maybe because of the scary implications. "Are people really free to do as they want?" they might have wondered. Who is going to hold back chaos? But God's plan does not abandon order, rather, once and for all, it establishes it. For, little did these doubters know about the illuminating power of God through the Holy Spirit, and the resulting acts of genuine love. Like I have said, grace is transforming. We obey because we love God! Some people marveled at the profundity of Jesus' message. And many believed.

Had the Jews heeded God's call in the words of Jesus, they could have been among his sheep. Instead, some sneered, asking questions about "the Christ," only wishing to catch Jesus in blasphemy. The miracles again spoke to reality, a reality that escaped their grasp. Jesus gives unblanketed assurance to his sheep and finishes by asking his accusers "For which of these (miracles) do you (presume) to stone me" (10: 32).

The evidence should have been overwhelming. But blindness persists. In the words of God through Isaiah was an astounding proclamation, "Be ever hearing, but never understanding; be ever seeing, but never perceiving. Make the hearts of this people calloused; make their ears dull and close their eyes. Otherwise, they might see with their eyes, hear with their ears, understand with their hearts, and turn and be healed" (Isaiah 6: 9-10).

Still, God, the ultimate gift giver, is calling today! Do you want to be healed?

CHAPTER 11

Darkness and Light

Jesus is light. His ability to raise Lazarus from the dead shows that he can also give life. The Pharisees are shrouded in darkness. They refuse to see, more concerned about their place of privilege and power.

Again, we have a reminder that not all tragedy and suffering are the result of sin. Indeed, sometimes it exists solely for the sake of glorifying God! How we respond, at any level of faith, can give testimony to God's goodness. God grants strength in trials, peace amidst turmoil, guidance in uncertainty, resolve in doubt, and comfort in grief. His way is demonstrably superior. And our lived testimonies have the potential to attract. In this story we will see how Jesus' power and presence transform Martha and Mary's tears into joy when Lazarus is raised from the dead. The miracle was as real as the stone moved back from the tomb. But like all of Jesus' miracles, they also serve as metaphors about God's ability to act in the world. Here, God restores life, or in our case invigorates an existence that has dried up like scattered bones.

The miracle happens in Bethany, just two miles from Jesus' troubles in Jerusalem. Jesus' disciples were concerned about his safety (11: 8). Jesus insists that we must continue working as long as there is light, which is as much a statement of purpose as there is for us today. As a backdrop, Jesus' hour of suffering and death is near, a reality of which he is fully aware. Still, he continues.

Remember, light and life are themes prevalent in John's Gospel; they go hand in hand. Jesus' insistence on the ability of light to keep one from stumbling is important. We have two choices--light versus darkness. Following light brings life! Following darkness brings spiritual death. For us, Jesus' example and teachings are light. When the light is followed, it brings vitality, wellbeing, and peace; this experience strengthens belief.

The disciples are confused by Jesus' language. Even Martha and Mary do not seem to entirely grasp what he is talking about. Notwithstanding, Jesus is deeply moved by Mary's tears. He even cries himself showing that he hurts when we hurt; he takes our situations personally.

Regardless of the coming miracle, knowledge of which might temper his emotion, Jesus feels empathy and compassion; he is not aloof. In contrast, today there are people so heavenly minded that they are no earthly good. Not Jesus. Absent are the shallow platitudes that skirt issues without appreciating their full impact. Absent are empty words of encouragement that only skim the surface of our deep inner state. God is with us; he knows. He took on flesh and experienced uncertainty. Yes, he shares our joys. But he also shares in our pain. He cheers when we succeed. And he grieves when we stumble.

Jesus raises Lazarus, and many put their faith in him. Yet, back in Jerusalem, the chief priests and Pharisees grumbled. They didn't appreciate him; they were only concerned with maintaining the status quo. They were the privileged, working to protect their place. So, they plotted to kill Jesus (11: 53).

CHAPTER 12

Jesus Receives His Rightful Due (Joy in Praise)

The anointing of Jesus' feet by Mary and the triumphal entry are proper responses to Jesus. Sadly, he is arrested and crucified just a week later. How fickle is human praise!

Mary's anointing of Jesus is as pure a display of tender devotion that we have in all of scripture. Her profound love is stunning. Surely, she was deeply moved, and her actions say far more than any formal creed can convey. It was a matter of the heart; genuine reverence and gratitude dripped like oil onto Jesus' feet. She carefully wiped his feet with her hair. Jesus' response is just as loving. He defends her against insincere gestures and legalistic responses with words that resounded with affirmation: "You will always have the poor among you, but you will not always have me" (12: 8). We can aspire to such devotion.

Next is the triumphal entry into Jerusalem where Jesus, again, receives what is due him. Remember, after the feeding of the five thousand they wanted to make him king. Now, after the raising of Lazarus, and after many other signs and wonders, they repeated this gesture. Excitement over the potential fulfillment of expectations, and joy, filled their hearts with the hopes for the coming age. The participants' souls overflowed enthusiastically. This was Palm Sunday, less than a week before his crucifixion. How fickle human praise is.

Jesus predicts his death with the explanation that a seed must first fall to the ground and be buried before it manifests an abundant return. Then he illumines a point for us to follow, "The man who loves his life will lose it, while the man who hates his life in this world will keep it for eternal life" (12: 25). Loving one's life entails grasping for any momentary happiness without any consideration for eternal things; we live to be pleased. Hating our lives, on the other hand, is shunning any expectations of personal benefit and relinquishing our prerogatives in the actions that follow. If you are solely motivated to receive, your intentions will be thwarted. But if instead, you act selflessly with the goals of showing and growing in love, expanding the principles of the kingdom of heaven, and glorifying God who is truly good, rewards abound. The apostle Paul calls this a baptism unto death where we die to our old greedy selves and emerge from the waters into newness of life (Romans (6: 4). Paramount, is the pledge of a clear conscience, and a commitment to change. Only then do we discover true joy, peace, wellbeing, wholeness, vitality, and love like has never been experienced before. I am not talking about a love that is merely duty, but feelings of love that satisfy the soul and direct the spirit. In God's economy of blessings, it is all about motivations. Align yourself with Him, and good things happen. Following the light, which is Christ, brings an abundance of life into this world, welling up to eternity. Find this, and you will truly be sons and daughters of light (12: 36).

"Even after Jesus had done all these miraculous signs in their presence, they still would not believe in him" (12: 37). This fact fulfilled the prophet Isaiah's words. Here, "He blinded their eyes and deadened their hearts" (12: 40), is not a statement about predestination. It is more a statement about how God is not going to force himself on anyone, and how continued stubbornness results in God turning you over to your own devises. He withdraws his presence, the presence of light itself. He allows choice where one reaps what one sows. I, personally, do not want to be left to my own propensities, for I have seen how bad that can be. I am afraid of being left to my own inclinations, apart from God's goodness, where there is only regret and misery. I have wandered in darkness and confusion, without life.

It is a good thing that, because of Jesus, God is just a prayer away. When I say that God withdraws his presence, I do not mean that he abandons you. Rather, he allows the dismal experience which you asked for with the intent of teaching you much needed lessons so that your faith might be strengthened and restored. One might be down, but not out. One might be lost, but there is always the potential of being found again. God is always present no matter how far we fall. It is just the matter of pointed involvement in bringing about blessings that is at stake. He then receives again those who repent, and in the end "gives us more grace." That is why Scripture says, "God opposes the proud but shows favor to the humble'" (James 4: 6). That is why many, though stubborn and resistant at first, were able to come to the point of sincere belief. Jesus, once experienced, is hard to reject.

CHAPTER 13

Nobody Is Greater Than His Master

Chapter 13 starts Jesus' final discourse with his disciples: important words. Lesson one is that nobody is greater than his master.

John dedicates the next five chapters of his Gospel to the night before his crucifixion. The scene is the Passover meal in a room set up for this occasion. The recipients of the message are only those closest to him. He offers encouragement and assurance before they are left to themselves. He tenderly exhorts and gives instruction for the coming days, weeks, months, and years. His ministry will be in their hands, guided by the Holy Spirit. If nothing else, know that these words are important. There are a total of twenty-one chapters and roughly one quarter of John's total account are devoted to this critical narrative in Jesus' life! You can hear in these chapters God speaking directly to you. He is encouraging you while preparing you for your faith journey.

Lesson one: "Very truly I tell you, no servant is greater than his master, nor is a messenger greater than the one who sent him" (13: 16). Jesus is our master; in comparison, we are insignificant. "Just as (Jesus) did not come to be served, but to serve" (Matthew 20: 28), our lives should reflect that purpose. Afterall, Jesus, our Lord and example, "who being in very nature God, did not consider equality with God something to be used to his own advantage; rather, he made himself nothing by taking the very nature of a servant, being made in human likeness. And being found in appearance as a man, he humbled himself by becoming obedient to death- even death on a cross" (Philippians 2: 6-8)! This is "the full extent of his love" (13: 1).

If Jesus suffered, we should expect to suffer at times as well. This is not a sign of condemnation, rather it is an honor and a privilege. Life can be hard. And as servants we should submit, knowing that in due time God will lift us up. Over and over in the Bible good things are promised to those who wait on the Lord. So, take heart. Be encouraged. And listen to instruction.

Underscoring this experientially, Christ proceeded to wash his disciples' feet. Recall the tenderness of Mary in her anointing of Jesus. This is even more tender. But Peter responds first with presumptuous humility, then naïve enthusiasm. Maybe he did not grasp the point. "'Do you understand what I have done for you,' Jesus asked them? 'You call me Teacher and Lord, and rightly so, for that is what I am. Now that I, your Lord, and teacher, have washed your feet, you also should wash one another's feet'" (13: 14).

Remembering that we are first and foremost servants, we cast off any imagined prerogatives and get about the business of tending to others. This can be a joy, but it can be a burden as well. Mourning with those who mourn is painful when we really experience other's predicaments. Putting ourselves in other's shoes can be tiresome and trying at best, and daunting at worse. Do not get discouraged, though, because God is with you. Tenderness shown today will come back as joy tomorrow. Keep your eyes on the horizon of God's love, and he will sustain you, repaying a thousand blessings for what you endure. In His time, God will answer with abundance if you only see others as Jesus did.

Immediately, Jesus predicts his betrayal. A prophecy is a strong affirmation of God's truth. The crux of this lies in acceptance, where anyone who receives the message also receives Christ, along with God the Father (13: 20). The fact that some reject the message troubles Jesus. Predominant among these is "the betrayer" himself (13: 21). Jesus discretely identifies him. But as Jesus intimated this to his disciples, Judas went out into darkness, the opposite of light.

Jesus' hour had come. The time of his glorification was at hand. For the disciples, Jesus needs to convey his message in its simplest form. A new command he gives, "Love one another. As I have loved you, so you must love one another" (13: 34).

John was very aware of all Jesus' teachings; like Matthew, he witnessed the Sermon on the Mount. Why is there no instruction in this Gospel about specifics? Maybe this is because he wanted to avoid our legalistic propensities. Love is simple. It is also broad. People could go to other places for rules. But the command to love encompasses them all. "By this all men will know that you are my disciples" (13: 35). An extra measure of grace is easy to identify, and it sums up all the Torah.

As to Jesus' destiny, Peter's bravado is revealing. "The spirit is willing, but the flesh is weak" (Matthew 26: 41). This represents so many of us; we want to do right but are unable. But for this too, Christ died. Like us, Peter would be overwhelmed with regret, maybe even shame. In our lives we can only get past it by comprehending the entire atoning work of Jesus.

CHAPTER 14

Comfort and Promises

Jesus comforts his beleaguered disciples with important words. The promise of salvation is important to one's strength. And the assurance of Christ being raised anticipates better things.

"Do not let your hearts be troubled" (14: 1). These are tender words to a group who is about to lose their most trusted friend. Sometimes things are so bad that all we can hope for is to see our loved one in heaven. For the disciples, Jesus himself is reassuring them of this coming reunion.

Hard times are coming. But the path should be clear. "I am the way and the truth and the life" (14: 6). "The way" can be taken in two senses. As to salvation, Jesus is the one who redeems us making it possible. As to the trajectory of their lives in this crisis, "the way" has been marked out in Jesus' words and deeds. His way is reliable; it is absolute truth. It is the truth about who we are and what we struggle with, about who we can become when we trust in the way, and about who Jesus is, namely the ultimate authority. "Life" can also be taken two ways. One form is eternal of which Jesus is our only hope. The other is temporal, potentially manifesting itself in vitality, strength, wellbeing, peace, love, and joy.

In Jesus, God is recognizable. The Father wants these things for us, so much that he sent his Son into the world as a solution to the problem of sin. Jesus and God are one.

The disciples should have already known this having lived with Jesus for "such a long time" (14: 9). If there is trouble with the concept, "at least believe on the evidence of the miracles themselves" (14: 11). Remember, God validated Jesus' ministry through many signs and wonders. These will be repeated in our lives through the moving of the mountains that we face.

Three times Jesus equates love for him with obedience; take that to heart. In the first instance he promises the Holy Spirit. This Counselor will live within the believer leading him to all truth. This Counselor assures that, in Jesus' absence, believers will not be left as orphans (14: 18). Cooperation with the Spirit results in sanctification. Maturity is the goal, which enables believers to thrive even in hard times. This is important when circumstances are tenuous. This side of the cross, it is important for us to imagine the ultimate good even when we may be dismayed. Afterall, a sincere witness is a strong testimony about the risen Christ. Vindication is at hand! A new day dawns.

In the second instance of obedience Jesus promises to show himself in personal ways. The word relationship is not used, but is implied by the three-way cohesion of Father, Jesus, and the believer. Personal means intimate, which is the way Christ reveals himself. Within the framework of an individual's thoughts and experience, attitudes to circumstances, and learned lessons, Jesus enters in ways you can relate to.

In the third instance of obedience the promise is that the Father and Jesus will make their home in the believer. They are recognizable in feelings of lasting exuberance. All three instances speak to an intimate bond. All three imply that guidance comes from above and resonates within the believer's heart. In essence, clarity, and conviction result from obedience. The implication is that one needs to look to the entirety of scripture to understand what acceptable behavior is.

"Peace, I leave with you; peace I give you. I do not give to you as the world gives. Do not let your hearts be troubled and do not be afraid" (14: 27). Again, tender words to a beleaguered group who must know that peace is the hallmark of the Christian life. Even in times of trial and tribulation, it remains. Like a warm blanket in the dead of winter, it keeps one feeling safe and warm. It settles deep into one's soul providing tranquility amidst chaos and confusion.

All this encouragement while on the brink of calamity ends with prophecy: "I have told you now before it happens, so that when it does happen you will believe" (14: 29). How gracious Christ is to protect us from doubt, assuring us that what we have with him is real regardless of the outcome. At the very least we will see him again in heaven. God only knows what the best for us will be.

CHAPTER 15

Jesus As the Vine

Lesson two: one must stay connected to Jesus to be fruitful in love. Away from his presence is frustration and burnout. In his Presence is joyful success.

Can you ensure another breath, or guarantee another day? Can you control the comings and goings of your world, or choose the people you will randomly run into? Can you create unforeseen opportunity, or avoid trial and limitations? God is over all! A measure of humility is reasonable, and we must be mindful of our dependency.

I felt for the longest time that God was always pruning me. By my experience, and by my eventually learning to prune myself, I thought that God intended somehow for me to be a gardener. My trials cropped up from deep within, and I felt the pain of always being cut back. But now I realize that God was forming me in my tribulations. He was revealing to me my weaknesses, my need for growth, my potential, and was ultimately developing in me lasting strength. He was preparing me to receive love, and once received, I could then give it. God was speaking to me. He told me that if I persist, I could feel the joy of being fruitful. He was also talking to me about sobriety, purity, faithfulness, and devotion. By myself I could gain no ground. But by remaining connected to the vine, opening myself up to being receptive, I inevitably grew.

Truth be told, you cannot force yourself to feel love. But by abiding, God instills love in you and you become fruitful. You cannot make yourself feel joy. But by abiding, God instills joy in you and you will be empowered with vitality.

Abiding or remaining is in essence active resting. God gives power and clarity to the one who responds. Clarity is a wonderful thing in that it brings joy. In this way, it is proved that God's word is alive and active in us. And we are rejuvenated.

Power to succeed is important. This success comes from a type of understanding which emanates from our most earnest efforts to submit to God's imploring us to taste that his ways are good. His truth resonates with our deepest being. It comes from experience and it invigorates. It motivates us to ever new heights.

So many people try to do it on their own and feel the pressure of what must be done to sustain it. The result is tedious labor in fields of thorns and thistles. People become grumpy, irritable, and discontent. People feel disillusionment. Misery marks their path, and depression sets in. From this vantage it is hard to share love let alone feel love. Life becomes a never-ending series of chores.

But Jesus beckons us to deeper waters. He urges us with the statement, "I have told you this so that my joy may be in you and that your joy may be complete" (15: 11). The command again is to love. And fruitfulness in love brings joy. But joy is not confined to love. It transforms into vitality to serve, and we soon discover that our deep-seated and sustained feelings of satisfaction are convincing marks of discipleship. They appear attractive to the outsider making people curious. They ensure fruitfulness, if we would only take heed.

Jesus abided in the Father's love. We must abide in Jesus' love. Jesus loved us so much that he laid down his life for us resolving the problem of sin, once and for all. The ultimate blessing is that we are going to heaven regardless of success in this world. It is reassuring to think that my salvation does not depend on me "getting it right," not the words that I speak nor the deeds that I do nor the understanding that I achieve. It is not by my mistakes, either, or my inabilities, or my misunderstandings that affect my eternal home. God knows that I am human, and he knows about all human limitations. He loves anyway, and is compassionate, so much so that he made a way despite all barriers. In our waning moments, while laying on our deathbeds, it really comes down to one thing, and that is Christ's love. We are completely dependent.

It would be unsettling had Christ's work not come with a promise. Of course, salvation would be enough to inspire worship and devotion. But God promises so much more--personal enrichment along with the power to succeed in this world if we would only abide.

Sadly, haters remain. But remember that they hated Christ first. We do not really belong to this world, so we have nothing to prove. Christ already validates us through our lives. So do not envy anyone. Remember, you are the one who feels joy and a sense of wellbeing. The haters reject Christ. Had he not come to show the way they would not be guilty. But by choosing their own course, despite him coming, they reject true joy, and their sin remains. Find comfort in prophecy: "They hated (Jesus) without reason" (15:25). And let God give you strength to carry on.

CHAPTER 16

The Work of the Holy Spirit

The work of the Holy Spirit in believers' lives grants success and encouragement. In the end, Christ wins.

At this very moment we can imagine Judas Iscariot conspiring with the religious leaders, Pharisees, and scribes. Jesus' purpose, his very destiny, awaits. Jesus' concern for his remaining disciples intensifies,

> All this I have told you so that you will not fall away. They will put you out of the synagogue; in fact, the time is coming when anyone who kills you will think they are offering a service to God. They will do such things because they have not known the Father or me. I have told you this, so that when their time comes you will remember that I warned you about them. I did not tell you this from the beginning because I was with you, but now I am going to him who sent me. None

> of you asks me, 'Where are you going?' Rather, you are filled with grief because I have said these things. But very truly I tell you, it is for your good that I am going away. Unless I go away, the Advocate will not come to you; but if I go, I will send him to you. When he comes, he will prove the world to be in the wrong about sin and righteousness and judgment: about sin, because people do not believe in me; about righteousness, because I am going to the Father, where you can see me no longer; and about judgment, because the prince of this world now stands condemned" (16: 1-11).

The remaining disciples appear bewildered. Without the Holy Spirit they do not have clarity. Evidently, he is coming. But how, and why, and where from? And what is this talk about going and coming? Do we really need a guide to truth? Afterall, we have you, Jesus.

Grief is coming. It will engulf the remaining disciples like a cloud. And then joy? Little do they know that Christ will be raised from the dead fulfilling all promises, proving that everything he said is true. This is about more than this life and our tedious affairs. It is about God demonstrating his love for all humanity! How we feel in this life seems insignificant in comparison. But is it? Experience indicates that this life is important. And our inner state has everything to do with how successful we will be in continuing Christ's ministry here on earth. The Holy Spirit will be our guide throughout all generations. Everything he teaches points to life.

The world offers empty promises. Pay no attention to what it sells. The world says you need "this" to be happy or try "that." The truth of the matter is that only God supplies what is truly needed. The world, however, hypes up its products trying to convince you that its way is best. But superficial distractions are all that it offers. Go down the world's road and you will soon see; nothing that it offers satisfies. In the end is disappointment and uncertainty, frustration and confusion, and dismay. Jesus imparts what is truly necessary; something lasting that wells up to eternity. The world does not care about you. It only succeeds in keeping you off balance.

Anything that asserts self and inflates pride is from the world. Anything that resembles greed or envy or lust is from the world. Superficial judgements and prejudice, temptations to self-medicate through drugs or alcohol, obsessions that press us to desire things beyond our finite human limitations are all from the world. The list goes on…

In contrast, when your heart sings while reading the Bible, that is from the Spirit. When the words of the Bible resonate with your experience, that is from the Spirit. When you realize that God is not as much giving rules as he is giving principles to apply, when you begin to be transformed by these principles, when you grow in the capacity to love, when you feel peace enough to be still or patient, when you are filled with life that wells up from inside, and when you feel with every fiber of your being that the God of the Bible is good, that is from the Spirit.

We cannot deny that in many ways the Spirit is subjective. Others may add what I leave out, and some may disagree with what I have listed. Discernment is key to life through the Spirit. And the more you heed God's call, the more clarity you will receive. Asking anything in Christ's name means being aligned with him. We might ask for a bunch of silly stuff if we were not on the same page. But as we grow, we pray only Godly prayers. And when we receive, our joy will be complete (16: 24).

The disciples indicate that at last, they see clearly, and not a moment too soon. "Do you now believe?" Jesus replied. "A time is coming and in fact has come when you will be scattered, each to your own home. You will leave me all alone. Yet I am not alone, for my Father is with me. I have told you these things, so that in me you may have peace. In this world you will have trouble. But take heart! I have overcome the world" (16: 31-33)!

CHAPTER 17

Jesus' Prayer for Us

This chapter focuses on this very powerful prayer.

Jesus ends this lengthy discourse with a prayer: "Father, the time has come. Glorify your Son, that your Son may glorify you" (17: 1). Father and Son, the two form an inextricable union. God glorifies the Son by vindicating everything about him on Easter Sunday making him the rightful focus of worship and praise. That Jesus endured severe suffering and death at the apex of his ministry underscores this point. Conversely, the Son glorifies the Father by revealing with open arms the very heart of God.

Who would have imagined that God would go the entire distance in bringing us back to him? Who would have thought that at the center of existence was unconditional love so extreme, so magnificent, that nothing could thwart this power's purpose? The revelation? God is a gift giver! And in the giving he does not circumvent justice but pays the price himself. The human dilemma of free will, sin, and suffering has been resolved. The plan, established before the foundation of the world, has been executed for all the world to see.

If the power of predestination exists in anyone, it miraculously existed in the experience of the Apostles. This ensured that they were "clean" (15: 3). Jesus nurtured them along by what Calvin identified as irresistible grace, and they responded. Obedience is a big part of this, like a horse responding to its rider's tug. Acceptance precedes obedience in that grasped knowledge of the truth is necessary before one is sure in taking their next step. First you see, feel, taste, smell, and hear, then you act. After living with Jesus some three years of his ministry, the Apostles believed God sent him. Their eventual witness would, in turn, glorify Jesus.

Again, we have the relational dynamic of being one. Being one with the Father ensures protection. Being one with each other brings joy. Sure, there will still be trials to endure, but with their minds set on heaven they will persevere. Like all Christians, the Apostles were merely pilgrims in this world. But it was in this world that they moved about in obedience to their mission.

"My prayer is not that you take them out of the world but that you protect them from the evil one" (17: 15). Here is acknowledgement that our ministry is to those in this world. Why some people insist on isolating themselves, I do not know. Maybe it is pain from repeated rejection.

Maybe it is the fear that this world engenders. Maybe it is fear about self. Shame could be a motivator, as could confusion and doubt. Whatever the case, as I mention it here with due respect, and a bit of curiosity, it seems likely and possibly ultimate that personal piety is placed above the command to love those who God himself has put in one's life.

But consider this before judging my observation: "Here is a trustworthy saying that deserves full acceptance: Christ Jesus came into the world to save sinners—of whom I am the worst" (1 Timothy 1: 15). If you are committed to being fruitful in love, you are going to get dirty. Life is messy, and it is in the trenches that battles are won. Ultimately, such close contact involves risk. That is why Jesus' prayer includes protection from the evil one. For sure, we must keep our wits about us. And we must not be deceived. Yet, it is by God's power through the Holy Spirit that victories are insured. But remember, we are all sinners first, thus the awesome wonder of the promise of salvation.

Success in these continual trials and temptations is what sanctifies us. Validating feelings of self-worth and contentment are discovered on the proving ground where the more you succeed, the more you will feel, and the less you succeed, the less you will feel. God always intended for us to grow from our mistakes.

The prayer crosses millenniums to today including all who believe. Many of the previous concepts are repeated.

Paramount is the theme of unity and oneness. Through this, people will see that Jesus is savior and people will see that Jesus is Lord.

Jesus ultimately wants to be with his disciples. And the promise of heaven looms large. But it is in this world that Jesus makes his mark. It is in this world that we believe and are transformed. And it is in this world, where we eat and breathe and move about, that God calls us to discipline and obedience.

CHAPTER 18

Jesus Arrested

Jesus arrested; the story of what he endured follows,

I will say it again; grace is transforming. It brings humility, then peace and joy and vitality and love. But at what cost. Isaiah reflects on this:

> "Who has believed our message and to whom has the arm of the Lord been revealed? He grew up before him like a tender shoot, and like a root out of dry ground. He had no beauty or majesty to attract us to him, nothing in his appearance that we should desire him. He was despised and rejected by mankind, a man of suffering, and familiar with pain. Like one from whom people hide their faces he was despised, and we held him in low esteem. Surely, he took up our pain and bore our suffering, yet we considered him

> punished by God, stricken by him, and afflicted. But he was pierced for our transgressions, he was crushed for our iniquities; the punishment that brought us peace was on him, and by his wounds we are healed" (53: 1-5).

Through Jesus, God grants a sense of wholeness and wellbeing. We have done nothing to deserve it, yet still he wants it for us. On the cross, it is there for the taking. Our ship has already come in. It has been in the harbor for generations.

John dedicates two succinct chapters to what transpired. There is more here than I could possibly articulate. Read them and see if you are not moved. I only offer what seems relevant to this book.

Some scholars speculate that Judas was motivated by nationalistic ideas about the Messiah. They believed that this "chosen one" was to restore Israel to a prominent state "here" in the present. The scholars contend that Judas believed that Jesus was indeed the Messiah and was merely trying to force Jesus' hand. Judas was disappointed at Jesus' lack of assertiveness. As a member of the insurrectionists, he intended to bring this conflict to a head "right now."

Even Peter's response of defense revealed intentions that were worldly. But Jesus rebuked him because he knew that his kingdom was not of this world (18: 36). The battle was spiritual, to be won or lost in the hearts of individuals throughout time. God would not force himself on anyone but would provide power and a way to commandeer life welling up to eternity. This is true life, to be accepted or rejected. On the cross and in the resurrection the line has been drawn in a spiritual battle of epic proportions.

Peter's denial of Christ is stunning; you would think that he should have seen it coming. I do not believe that it was a matter of heart. More likely, it shows how sin sneaks up on us in the details of our lives. We all deny Christ in many ways. Often it is a reflex of circumstance. We focus on one thing, then something else surprises us. There are reasons why we justify our actions. Some things seem more immediate than the rest. Peter was so focused on being there, which required a sort of secrecy, that the consequences of his words eluded his conscious grasp. We too are guilty of the same mistake. Only Peter's sin preceded the antidote. It would be a short time before forgiveness would be revealed. But for days he would have to bear feelings of regret and despair.

Some people deny the battle through relativism. Like Pilot, they shrink into conversations about subjectivity and perspective. "What is truth" (18: 38), they say skeptically, while disappearing into the backdrop of a bigger story, as if Christ did not prove to be King, as if the Way and the truth and the Light were not as solid as the very ground they stand on. This relativism chooses sinking sand. It fades into oblivion like smoke from a candle in a dark room. But the battle rages on. And Christ promises the energy of hope for all who believe.

CHAPTER 19

A Sad Parody on Authority

The King of all creation stands condemned.

The steady escalation of threats and posturing against an innocent man by the religious leaders and Pharisees and scribes, or those in power, had reached a crescendo in chapter 18. Evidently, Jesus was too popular, a fact that threatened the leader's place of prestige and privilege. This led to an arrest and interrogation, first before Annas, then Caiaphas, then Pilot who represented the Roman Empire. There are a number of political factors involved, with everyone looking out for themselves. The call is to crucify or get rid of the trouble.

The whole drama is a sad parody on authority, where things are turned on their heads and grotesquely skewed. The world's representatives exert themselves over and above the ultimate authority, God himself. It started with an unjust strike to Jesus's face (18: 22). A crown of thorns and a mocking purple robe led to a flogging (19: 5). Irritated by Jesus' quiet submissiveness, Pilot utilizes his point of leverage. "Jesus answered, 'You would have no power over me if it were not given to you from above'" (19: 11). These words are a scolding testament against any successful person who thinks that his accomplishments are a reason for pride. What does anyone have that God did not supply? Intellect, talent, drive, appeal? God grants it all. Still, in chapter 19, the King of the universe, the ultimate authority on true life and living, the very fountainhead of all things good, stands condemned.

Scourging is a more accurate word for what Jesus endured. A scourge is a multi-stranded whip with glass, nails, and stones tied to its ends so that a lash from it tore at the flesh of the recipient. By the end of the scourging, disfigured beyond recognition, Jesus was already near death. Imagine the anguished pain, the torture, the torment Christ felt while carrying his own cross. They then drove nails through his hands and feet pinning him to the wooden planks of the cross. Utterly depleted from the trauma, and dehydrated beyond belief, Jesus said "I am thirsty" (19: 28). "When he had received the drink," he murmured softly, "It is finished." And he bowed his head and released his spirit (19: 30).

At this point in the Gospel of Matthew the earth shook, and the temple curtain was torn from top to bottom (27:

51). This was a profound indication that salvation, access, and life are ultimately God's work from start to finish. Jesus succeeded in doing for us that which we cannot do for ourselves. Perfectly, he bore our burdens and freely died for our faults, taking our place in punishment, and offering new life through him.

At this point in the Gospel of Luke the earth went dark (23: 44). The light of this world had been rejected and discarded, snuffed out like a candlewick. The centurion on duty, after seeing these things exclaimed, "Surely, this was a righteous man" (23:47). I imagine others looking on with astonishment wondered, "God, what are you doing up there?"

"One of the soldiers pierced Jesus' side with a spear, bringing a sudden flow of blood and water. The man who saw it has given testimony, and his testimony is true. He knows that he tells the truth, and he testifies so that you also may believe" (19: 34-35)!

Carefully, John weaves prophecy throughout his account. In relevant moments he inserts scripture giving us perspective and hope. Who, but God, can predict the future and bring it about? All along, Jesus had spoken candidly about this day. Not until after did people remember and understand, praising God for this remarkably compassionate deed of mercy and grace.

Remember Nicodemus? He is here at the end. Possibly, his faith has matured, and he has found true life; he has been born of the Spirit. He brings a mixture of myrrh and aloes to help Joseph of Arimathea prepare Jesus' body for burial. "At the place where Jesus was crucified, there was a garden, and in the garden a new tomb, in which no one had ever been laid. Because it was the Jewish day of Preparation and since the tomb was nearby, they laid Jesus there" (19: 41-42).

CHAPTER 20

Vindication!

Jesus is raised from the dead, proving all that he promised is true.

God's powerful victory on Easter morning brings awesome joy! Feelings of love spring forth in those who have seen. There is a sense of wellbeing and wholeness like never before. There is vitality and peace, and the strength to carry on.

God brings clarity and purpose even in desperate situations. His presence instills exuberance and courage to face another day. Imagine Mary Magdaline's delight in seeing the risen Lord. Her teacher, friend, and confidante had returned to restore all things.

At first, though, Mary is uncertain. She runs to tell the disciples that the tomb is empty. They, in turn, run to see for themselves. Sure enough, it is just as she said. But what does this mean?

Mary stays by the tomb. Alone, she cries. Then angels appear declaring the truth; this, right before Jesus stands in her presence. At first, she does not recognize him, but he tenderly calls her by name. Christ's personal and intimate address to Mary revealed his presence. He knows us to our core, and supplies what we need. Mary recognizes him, and at once holds on with reverent devotion. Jesus instructs her to be a witness to the disciples. With enthusiasm, she does what she is told.

The disciples do not have to wait long for verification. That same night, Jesus disperses their fears and doubts by appearing among them behind doors that were locked for fear of the Jews. Remember, Jesus does not give as the world gives; he gives peace. And he breathed the Holy Spirit into them. "As the Father has sent me, I am sending you" (20: 21). They will be witnesses to true life, present and eternal.

Thomas was not there that night, so he still had doubts. But Jesus graciously meets his needs by appearing again, offering a feel of his hands and side. "Thomas said to him, 'My Lord and my God!' Then Jesus told him, 'Because you have seen me, you have believed; blessed are those who have not seen and yet have believed'" (20: 28-29). Here is the promise that traverses the millenniums. The message about both experiences of believing come directly to us. God frees captives and gives gifts even in our time. If we only believe.

I would have fainted had I not believed that I would see the goodness of the Lord in the land of the living (Psalm 27: 13 KJV). But I have seen it and believe. All those years of anguish and distress are forever gone. Now, joy lifts my step, and peace adorns my path. Like a newborn baby, I crave pure spiritual milk, so that by it I may grow up in Christ's salvation, now that I have tasted that the Lord is good (1 Peter 2: 2-3). Follow Jesus as the Way and the Truth and the Life, and you will see too. Commit your life to him as Lord and Savior. And he, the good shepherd, will provide and make a way for you!

CHAPTER 21

"Follow Me"

This chapter provides a description of what following Jesus entails.

A frustrated fishing trip was turned into a bounty at Jesus' suggestion. "This was now the third time Jesus appeared to his disciples after he was raised from the dead" (21: 14). Like in many of these appearances, Jesus' identity was shrouded. Here in chapter 21, they thought that they recognized him, but dared not ask (21: 12). Earlier, Mary mistook Jesus for a gardener before he addressed her by name (20: 15-16). In the Gospel of Luke, on the road to Emmaus, two unsuspecting travelers walk for miles with Jesus unaware of who he is (Luke 24: 13-35).

It makes one wonder if we would recognize Jesus today. Hard to tell, but one thing is certain. In the Gospel of Matthew Jesus says, when we feed the hungry, give drink to the thirsty, invite a stranger, clothe the needy, and visit the sick and imprisoned, we do that to Christ

(Matthew 25: 37-40). Christ is in the eyes of the oppressed, the hearts of those who mourn, the tears of those who are broken, the sweat of the poor, and the bowed heads of the meek. It is up to us to recognize him, and lay hold of every opportunity to serve.

For the two on the road to Emmaus, after recognizing that they had been with Jesus, they reflected, "were not our hearts burning within us while he talked with us on the road and opened the Scriptures to us" (Luke 21: 32)? We might ask a similar question after tending to the needy, "were not our hearts burning with love in that sacred moment of compassion?"

Back to the miraculous catch of fish received at Jesus' beckoning, on the shore where flays had been cooking above a fire started by Jesus himself, Jesus confronts Peter. "Do you love me?" he asked three times, one for every denial of Peter just one week prior. Peter answered "yes" to all three questions, his trembling voice intensifying with each instance. "Tend to my sheep," Jesus said on all three accounts (21: 15-17).

Closely related in intent is a verse in Luke: "Simon, Simon, Satan has asked to sift you as wheat. But I have prayed for you, Simon, that your faith may not fail. And when you have turned back, strengthen your brothers" (Luke 22: 31-32).

One can imagine Peter's remorse after he had failed miserably at the house of the high priest on the night on which Jesus was betrayed. Who knows how long he suffered, and how deep he sank into despair after that regretful occasion. But God does not despise a broken spirit, and a broken and contrite heart (Psalm 51: 17). So, Jesus prays for Peter.

In essence, Jesus might have tenderly quoted Isaiah: "Forget the former things; do not dwell on the past. See, I am doing a new thing! Now it springs up, do you not perceive it" (Isaiah 43: 18-19)? Shame, doubt, and fear are powerful emotions that debilitate us and keep us down. Only after we get past them by opening ourselves up to what Jesus is doing, does the bud of love spring up in our hearts allowing the possibility of restored usefulness. Remember, "Great is his faithfulness; his mercies begin afresh each morning" (Lamentations 3: 23).

Back to the miraculous catch, the breakfast meal, and the confrontation of Peter. Jesus and he are walking along the shore when Jesus stops Peter short with a prophecy: for the glory of God, Peter will become a martyr (21: 18-19). Peter turned and saw John who was following. "What about him?" Peter asked (21: 21). In essence, Jesus said something like never you mind about him; just follow me (21: 22).

I am reminded of all the conflict and division that there is in the church over who is really going to heaven. I, personally, do not busy my mind with such thoughts. I, for one, take Paul's advice found in Romans: "Do not say in your heart, 'who will ascend into heaven?' (that is, to bring Christ down) or 'who will descend into the deep?' (that is, to bring Christ up from the dead). But what does it say? The word is near you; it is in your mouth and in your heart, that is, the word of faith we are proclaiming: That if you confess with your mouth, "Jesus is Lord," and believe in your heart that God raised him from the dead, you will be saved" (Romans 10: 6-10).

"But what about him?" people ask. "He's not sincere!" or "he's not trying hard enough!" or "he did this!" or "he did not do that!" The resounding census seems to be "He's a sinner!" But is not that the point. We are all sinners, lost in our own perspectives and rationales, blind to our own motives, prisoners of our own unwieldy drives. The miracle is that by the One powerful act of mercy and grace we are forgiven! Heaven is guaranteed!

In the meantime, it is this world that becomes important. I can either feel joy, or I can be miserable. I can have vitality or feel dejected and downhearted. I can have a sense of wellbeing and wholeness, or I can be empty inside. I can feel peace, or I can be anxious. Christ freed us! Now enjoy your freedom.

Jesus' advice to Peter was basically stay in your own lane. "I have given you gifts, blessings, and abilities, so just concentrate on using them." If you want to know what brings joy, heed Jesus' call, Justice, equality, fairness, respect, grace through gentleness, kindness, and humility bring joy. If you want to know misery, be oppressive, mean-spirited, hateful, selfish, prejudiced, proud, insensitive, greedy, and lustful, the list goes on.

It is a new day! Be transformed by the renewing of your mind (Romans 12: 2). Cultivate goodness into your heart. Do some soul-searching. Learn to be genuine; the same inside as out. Make good choices by following the Holy Spirit. Listen to Jesus. And follow his path knowing all the while that eternal springs are waiting for you, ready to fill your cup to overflowing.

Epilog Lessons from Abraham

Patience and proper motivations are key.

Abraham was seventy-five years old when God promised him a prodigy and a land inheritance. Though he was aged, and his prospects seemed futile, he believed, and it was reckoned to him as righteousness. It was twenty-five more years before the promise was fulfilled. In that time, he struggled with doubt. Just think, twenty-five years of silence. He occasionally tried by his own means to bring the promise to fruition. He floundered in attempts of self-preservation and self-realization.

Abraham was a person just like us. We too stagger and fall, lose our way, then are brought back. The first point is that no matter how futile things may seem, just believe. Believe that God loves you. Believe he cares about your struggles and future. Believe he will make a way. Believe that he already has through the atoning work of Jesus, and that your eternal destiny is secure.

I was forty years old when I first gave my life to Christ. Just think, forty years in the desert of mistakes, causing harm, and being harmed. The message of forgiveness was attractive. Immediately upon my commitment to Jesus I felt peace, contentment, a sense of wellbeing and happiness. But it was ten more years before I first encountered Christian joy.

Now, I experience Christian joy as the vitality and confidence needed to love in all circumstances, the ability to differentiate myself from the confusion of perspectives which surround me while finding the common good, and an appreciation of the differences in people that I now respect, giving me true affection for them. Joy is the energy behind relationship. Joy is the humor amidst the mundane. Joy is fresh each morning and alive and active.

The question is, why did it take so long for me to discover it? Well, there were the ten years of legalistic attempts to earn my place. I was taking care of all the details, watching my P's and Q's so to speak while cultivating the soil of my soul. This was all good on many levels, and for sure I learned a lot and was growing. But truth be told, I was not listening to what God was talking directly to me about. Sure, I still had lots of flaws. But God was not talking to me about those. Instead, He was speaking loudly and plainly to me about sobriety. And it was ten more years before I finally surrendered.

My life took off! Joy, vitality, strength, endurance, wellbeing, peace, and wholeness took hold to sustain me in fruitfulness. My complaint had been that I was turning into a grumpy old man. Discontentment, bitterness, irritation, and the lack of patience marked my walk. Then I prayed, "God, help me feel love and I will quit drinking." I finally quit, and God answered.

God gives clarity. He can make sense of your life, showing you how your mistakes came about within the details of your existence. "The most excellent way" awaits (1 Corinthians 13). It is profoundly personal. God knows you intimately, better than you do yourself. God is both transcendent and near. His wisdom is way up there beyond comprehension. Yet, it is right here, accessible to all.

Issac was born when Abraham was one hundred years old. Oh, the joy on that day! Issac grew in stature, evidence that the promise had sustaining power. Then God asked something dreadful of Abraham: present your beloved son as a sacrifice. Abraham must have felt horrified and dejected. But if God had taken him this far, he would surely see things through to completion.

The site of the sacrifice was in the region of Moriah; the name of the specific mount was called "The Lord will provide." The test, or the question, was "do you love the gift more than the giver?" God never intended for Issac to die. It was Abraham's heart which was being revealed.

At some point, we might face a similar test. For now, God keeps us in our joy. He sustains it, but as the Lord gives, he can also take away. Granted, there is purpose. Yet, the dreadful prospect of misery remains a possibility.

I catch glimpses of it here and there in days when I just do not "feel it." In those, though they may be few, I simply concentrate on obedience, for I have learned that God's way is best. Remaining constant and firm is important to me. The ability to wait on the Lord is a skill necessary for success. But in these moments the question remains, "if I never experienced joy again, would I still praise God?" or, in practice, "Do I love the gift more than the giver?"

God's presence brings joy. When he feels distant to me, I understand that it is not he who has moved, but me. On these occasions I return to the cross where doubts evaporate, anxiety is soothed, and humility is rekindled. I become settled in the conviction that it is not by my successes in life that I am saved; it is by Christ's mercy, love, and grace. The promise is for everyone, no matter how blind, no matter how stubborn, no matter how lost. In the end, it is God's love that perseveres.

I pray that I will die well. And a part of me longs for that day of eternal rest. God's perfect presence brings that rest. It pervades heaven, where there will be perfect community. In this world there will be trouble. And when we see rightly, we realize that suffering is not as much a dilemma as a circumstance to be overcome. This is not heaven. If it was, there would be no suffering. This is the proving ground where faith is matured in the fires of trial and error. Perfection awaits.

In Romans, in contemplating the infusion of all Isreal into the Kingdom of God, Paul marvels at the mystery of all-inclusive saving grace. In this instance he considers with joy the incoming of all his people together under God's care. We can convey that to our world with joy.

> Oh, the depth of the riches of the wisdom and knowledge of God! How unsearchable his judgements, and his paths beyond tracing out: who has known the mind of the Lord? Or who has been his counselor? Who has ever given to God, that he should repay him? For from him and through him and to him are all things. To him be the glory forever! Amen" (11: 33-36).

How expansive is God's love? We stand in awe and wonder. Our finite minds cannot possibly comprehend his purposes and majesty. All we can do is submit to his wisdom proclaiming God's love through Jesus Christ our Lord, and experience the joy!

A Call to Unity (and Joy)

Enemy is a strong word loaded with harsh pitfalls. We have lived together so long, have stood on the same side, have felt and shown affection and respect. Ultimately, we are brothers and sisters. We have shared love.

The current political environment is challenging. It has raised concerns about division. Allegiances are becoming polarized. And the farther we progress, the wider the chasm has become. The consequences, or results, of holding a particular view has never in my memory been so prominently displayed on the evening news. Real lives are being destroyed. Real families are being hurt. And this is only on the local level.

World relationships are in upheaval. Within America, the very founding principles of life, liberty, and justice for all are being violated. "We the people" seem to be irretrievably lost. We stand on opposite sides of an ideological chasm.

May I suggest that it might be necessary in effectively negotiating the times that "all" take a good dose of humility in dealing with circumstances that are way bigger than any one person. We need to respect others in their ability to make sense of the world, to answer the big questions which are at the seat of conviction, to find and defend truth. We need to start a conversation where people truly listen and learn. And we need to speak calmly and compassionately regarding our own experiences. We need to adequately assess our own flaws, blind spots, and inabilities while considering the whole. While questioning what it means to be human, we need to rally in solidarity as equal partakers of humanity, identifying our common struggles as well as our dreams. A good measure of grace will be required. And mercy should be at the heart of any call to come together. In viewing the circumstances as they stand two questions remain. Like the first century Pharisees, religious leaders, and scribes, has our religion made us hard-hearted, and are we chasing the law at the expense of love?

The existence of evil in the world, a force that is recognizable, is evidence against theories of relativism. There is a physical reality "out there" which stands apart from all rationalizations which need to be addressed. God judges the heart, and only his judgements are just. Knowing that God cares about justice and will rectify grievances helps me stand amidst the chaos of the world. I am relieved that the burden of judgement is in capable hands. God never meant for any one of us to bear it by ourselves. So, starting out, I surrender my worries and fears to God, which may be a prerequisite of becoming something useful: "Blessed are the meek, for they will inherit the world" (Matthew 5: 5).

Breaking news: God is not restricted by our interpretations of the Bible. We are finite in understanding, and we are flawed. God, on the other hand, is infinite and good. He will have mercy on whom he will have mercy. And He will show compassion on whom he will show compassion. It is comforting to know that God accepts a contrite heart and a broken spirit. The choice is ours today! In a situation which engulfs us let us approach the throne of God with humility. Let us seek first the kingdom of heaven and trust that God will honor our request for guidance by creating something good. For the sake of everyone's personal wellbeing, let us then chose the good. Let us choose God! Salvation is at hand. There will be joy in the end.

www.ingramcontent.com/pod-product-compliance
Lightning Source LLC
LaVergne TN
LVHW010931110826
845149LV00013B/2550

9781957354903